P9-EDR-156

Basic Beauties

Easy Quilts for Beginners

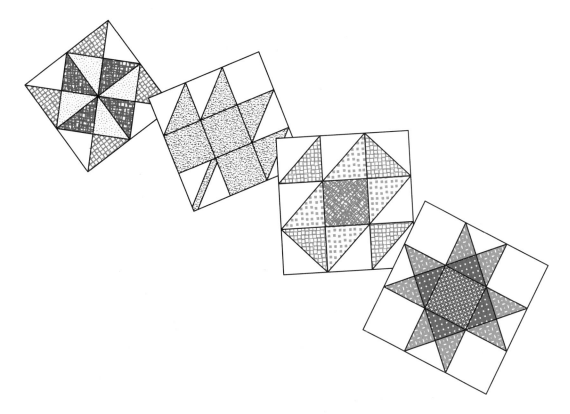

Eileen Westfall

That Patchwork Place®

Credits

Editor-in-Chief .... Barbara Weiland
Technical Editor .... Janet White
Managing Editor .... Greg Sharp
Copy Editor .... Liz McGehee
Proofreader .... Leslie Phillips
Design Director .... Judy Petry
Text and Cover Designer .... Dani Ritchardson
Production Assistant .... Shean Bemis
Illustrators .... Laurel Strand
                                                          Carolyn Kraft
Illustration Assistant .... Lisa McKenney
Photographer .... Brent Kane

Basic Beauties
© 1995 by Eileen Westfall
That Patchwork Place, Inc., PO Box 118, Bothell, WA
98041-0118 USA

Printed in the United States of America
00 99 98 97 96 95   6 5 4 3 2 1

Library of Congress Cataloging-in-Publication Data
Westfall, Eileen.
    Basic beauties : easy quilts for beginners / Eileen Westfall.
        p. cm.
    IBSN 1-56477-098-2
        1. Quilting—Patterns. 2. Patchwork—Patterns. 3. Quilted goods.
I. Title.
TT835.W4787 1995   95-4037
746.46—dc20   CIP

Dedication

This book is dedicated to my mother, Lila Kurth Stone, who put the first needle in my hand and taught me how to sew.

Acknowledgments

Thanks go to: Jeanette Baird for quilting the Leaves of the Seasons quilt, Katherine Bilton for quilting the Needles and Spools and Grandmother's Fan quilts, Betty Hershberger for quilting the Stars and Stripes quilt, Leslie Pease for quilting the Four Log Cabins quilt, and Cricket Hamilton for taking the author's photograph.

No part of this product may be reproduced in any form, unless otherwise stated, in which case reproduction is limited to the use of the purchaser. The written instructions, photographs, designs, projects, and patterns are intended for the personal use of the retail purchaser and are under federal copyright laws; they are not to be reproduced by any electronic, mechanical, or other means, including informational storage or retrieval systems, for commercial use.

The information in this book is presented in good faith, but no warranty is given nor results guaranteed. Since That Patchwork Place, Inc., has no control over choice of materials or procedures, the company assumes no responsibility for the use of this information.

MISSION STATEMENT

WE ARE DEDICATED TO PROVIDING QUALITY PRODUCTS THAT ENCOURAGE CREATIVITY AND PROMOTE SELF-ESTEEM IN OUR CUSTOMERS AND OUR EMPLOYEES.

WE STRIVE TO MAKE A DIFFERENCE IN THE LIVES WE TOUCH.

That Patchwork Place is an employee-owned, financially secure company.

Table of Contents

Introduction

Welcome to the wonderful world of Quilting! If you are like many beginning quilters I have talked to, you have probably been thinking about learning this creative craft for some time. Quilts are all around us to admire; they pop up in magazines, movies, and on TV. Most everyone has a quilt made by an aunt or a grandmother, and often, these quilts have an interesting story.

Quilting is fascinating because there are so many design possibilities. Thousands of traditional patchwork patterns are in print and more new patterns are created each year. Today, with the passionate revival of quilting in full swing, there are endless resources available to the quilter: books, magazines, clubs, and wonderful fabric stores for quilters only.

Basic Beauties is a book designed for you, the novice quilter. All the quilts have been taken from traditional patterns and adapted with a few fresh twists. They are presented in a simple, step-by-step format with illustrations for each step to help you make your first quilting project successful. Quilting is addictive, as any quilter will attest. I am sure, once you have completed your first masterpiece, you will be eager to go on to the next and the next!

This is a book of easy designs specifically for beginning quilters. There are at least three ways to use this book, depending on the size of the projects you want to make:

1. Make the complete project as shown in the picture.
2. Take one block design from any project and make it into a pillow. (See "Making a Pillow" on page 21.)
3. Take one block design from any project and make a tote bag. (See "Making a Tote Bag" on page 23.)

Though there are twelve basic projects, you can make many more than those twelve basics:

    12 quilts
    21 pillows
    21 tote bags

That totals fifty-four possible projects.

If the thought of a whole quilt scares you, start with a pillow or a tote. Once you have successfully made the smaller item, you can go on to the larger ones without anxiety.

You might want to start off with one of the complete projects. You will find all the step-by-step information you need in this book.

Project Elements

All projects in this book include a list of supplies you will need, a cutting guide for the projects, and complete directions. Full-size templates are included for projects that require them, and all projects have detailed illustrations to help you every step of the way.

All fabrics and materials to make the projects are listed under "Materials" in each quilt plan. Tools not mentioned in the quilt plans are listed under Basic Equipment below.

Most cotton fabric is 44" to 45" wide. After washing, the usable width of the fabric may be no more than 42". The yardage amounts listed are based on that width. If the fabric you use isn't 42" wide after washing, you may have to make some adjustment to the amounts listed in the quilt plans to be sure you have enough to make the projects.

The cutting guide for each project lists all the pieces that you cut from fabric and other materials, including batting. It can be helpful to cut all the pieces ahead of time.

Quiltmaking Basics

Basic Equipment

For best results, you need to have some good basic equipment. This section lists everything you need to make the projects.

Glue Sticks

Because they have a waxy base, glue sticks are neat, clean, and easy to use, which makes them ideal for holding fabric shapes in place for appliqué. Check the label on your glue stick to be sure it can be used on fabric.

Light Box

A light box is a handy piece of equipment for marking quilting, embroidery, and other designs on fabric. It provides a light source behind the pattern and the piece of fabric so you can mark design lines easily.

Light boxes have low, rectangular frames that come in a wide range of sizes. Some are as small as 12" x 10", with a smooth, translucent top surface and one or more bulbs or tubes inside for illumination.

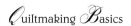

Marking Pens

Erasable marking pens are available with two different kinds of ink: one kind fades with time, the other washes out with water. Each type has advantages and disadvantages.

Fading-ink pens make light marks that may fade before a project is completed, which means you may need to mark the piece again. I use fading-ink markers only on small projects that I know will be completed quickly.

The other type of ink, which washes out with water, is usually a bright color. Traces may reappear after drying. Fabrics may have to be washed many times before the markings disappear completely.

Needles and Pins

You will need general sewing needles for sewing openings in the projects and embroidery needles for the embroidered details on a few of the projects.

Quilting needles are essential, as most of the projects involve quilting. Quilting needles are usually labeled "Betweens." A package of quilting needles, or Betweens, may contain an assortment of needle sizes from size #7 to size #12. The higher the number, the finer and shorter the needle, with #12 being the finest. Despite seeming difficult to handle at first, the smaller the needle, the easier it is to make tiny, neat quilting stitches.

Be sure you always use the best pins available, even if they seem expensive. Dull pins can snag the fabric and are difficult to use. Silk pins and ball-tip pins are the sharpest and glide through the fabric smoothly. Many of these pins have round, colored heads. As someone who has been stuck by many stray pins, I highly recommend this type for their ease of use as well as their visibility.

Quilting Tape

The projects that involve quilting will be easier if you use quilting tape as you quilt. Quilting tape is a paper tape (also known as masking tape) that is available in quilting shops.

It comes in various widths, as narrow as $\frac{1}{16}$".

The tape is applied directly to the item being quilted as a stitching guide, so that your lines of stitching will be perfectly straight. Quilting tape is relatively inflexible, so it is not suitable for outlining curves.

Don't leave the tape on your quilt for extended periods of time as it can leave a residue that is difficult to remove.

Rotary Cutters

The rotary cutter is a cutting implement that features a circular blade. For safety when not in use, it has a protective shield that slides out beyond the blade. Rotary cutters are available in a variety of sizes and are made by several different manufacturers.

Rotary-Cutting Mat

Rotary-cutting mats come in many different shapes and sizes. They are made from a material that is somewhat impervious to the cuts of a rotary cutter and lasts for years.

Make sure your mat is printed with a 1" grid and that the outer grid lines are divided into $\frac{1}{8}$" increments. They will make your cutting easier and more accurate. Be sure your mat also has diagonal lines running across the grid to help you when you are cutting bias strips.

Rulers

You will also need special rulers that have inches marked both vertically and horizontally. The first ruler I recommend for beginners is 18" long and 3" wide. You will also need a 6" Bias Square® ruler. Several other rulers are helpful for advanced techniques, but these will do for beginning-level projects.

Scissors

It is important to keep a separate pair of scissors for cutting fabric only. Have additional pairs on hand for cutting paper and other materials. Be sure to keep all of your scissors sharp, so that cutting goes as smoothly as possible.

Seam Rippers

In a craft as exacting as patchwork, mistakes are hard to avoid. If you make a mistake, don't get discouraged. So long as you correct your errors neatly, no harm is done.

If a seam needs to be taken out and restitched, use a seam ripper to reduce your frustration. Slip the point of the seam ripper under a stitch, pushing forward and pulling up to break the thread. Work along the seam, breaking every third or fourth stitch. When you come to the end of the seam, carefully pull the two pieces of fabric apart. They should separate easily. Remove the thread from the unstitched seam and restitch.

Sewing Machines

Every project in this book requires the use of a sewing machine. Make sure yours is in working order and has been oiled recently before you begin sewing. I own an inexpensive, no-frills sewing machine that makes only straight or zigzag stitches. It isn't computerized, and it doesn't do a multitude of decorative stitches, but it's a great sewing machine and does all I need to do for my quilting projects.

Sewing Machine Needles

Start each project with a new needle, using a size appropriate for sewing cotton fabric. Make sure the new needles will fit your machine before buying.

Thimbles

I have a confession to make. In the many years that I have been sewing, I have never felt comfortable using a thimble. I am left-handed, and I do many things upside down or backwards, which could be the source of what I call my "thimble block."

I have tried every kind of thimble made, even the soft leather ones, but I have never found one that was really comfortable, so I work without a thimble. Do yourself a favor and use one if you can. A thimble will protect your fingers, push the needle more easily through the fabric, and you will enjoy painless sewing and quilting.

Thread

In my early days of sewing, I made a yellow patchwork item and used navy blue thread to stitch it together. I didn't have any yellow thread on hand at the time, and I wasn't aware that it would be a mistake to use contrasting color thread. The navy blue that I used showed through and gave the item an overall dingy look. I learned an important lesson from that project: always use sewing thread that matches the fabric!

Color

Everyone has favorite colors—colors that they tend to choose. Color is as important to a project as the design. It plays a large part in whether or not an item is aesthetically pleasing. I have used colors I like for the projects in this book. You will want to exercise your own preferences. Some basic color information may help you make your choices.

Colors, Tones, Tints, and Shades

There are three primary colors, the colors from which all other colors are derived: yellow, red, and blue. The secondary colors are orange, violet, and green. The tertiary colors are yellow-orange, red-orange, red-violet, blue-violet, blue-green, and yellow-green.

White, black, and gray do not appear on the color wheel and are not considered colors.
- A tint results when white is added to a color.
- A shade results when black is added to a color.
- A tone results from adding gray to a color.

Color Values

Value is the lightness or darkness of a color. Tints are light or high in value, and shades are dark or low in value.

I prefer a formula of dark colors for the dominant pieces in my blocks, medium colors for the secondary pieces, and light colors for the background pieces. This formula can also be effective in reverse: light values for domi-

nant pieces, medium values for secondary pieces, and dark values for background pieces. Amish quilts typically display this reverse color-value scheme.

Color Schemes

There are three main types of color schemes: monochromatic, analogous, and complementary.

- A monochromatic scheme consists of shades or tints of the same color.
- An analogous scheme combines related colors, those that are next to each other on the color wheel.
- A complementary scheme brings together colors that are opposite each other on the color wheel.

Remember that your color choices send as strong a message as the design itself. Take a minute to determine what message you want your piece to project. Study the color wheel and learn what colors work well together. Look through books and magazines at pictures of almost anything. Note the color combinations and ask yourself if they are pleasing to your eye. Do some experimenting and play with scraps of colored fabric, laying them side by side to see how they look. Many quilters have a design wall or board covered with flannel to use for color "scheming."

To make a design wall, cut a large piece of fleece or thin batting and use masking tape or push pins to attach it to the wall. Then play with patchwork patches on the fleece. The patches will adhere to the fleece, much like a flannel board.

Fabric

Many quilters love to amass great quantities of fabric so that they will have some on hand when a creative idea strikes them. Then they get an idea for a new project and go out to buy new fabric for the new project. I wonder how many thousands of yards of fabric, lying in closets all over the world, will never be used!

Whatever your philosophy of fabric buying, here are a few of my thoughts about the fabric for the projects in this book. Several of the projects can be made from very little fabric. I keep color-keyed bags of scraps in my studio for small projects. I use self-sealing plastic bags and put as many pieces of one color in each bag as I can. That way, when I am making a small project and looking for the right color fabric, I have a chance of finding what I need without making a trip to the fabric store. I keep all of my scraps in a box. I think it's fun to keep scraps of truly wonderful fabric and a challenge to use them in a second or even a third project.

Wash all fabric before beginning a project. Eliminate shrinkage before cutting and stitching, not after a project is completed.

I recommend that you use only 100% cotton fabric for all your quilting projects. Polyester and polyester blends pucker and pull, and they don't give the fine results that all-cotton fabric does. Check the end of the bolt to be certain of the fabric content when you purchase material. If you have pieces at home that you are not sure about, try the two methods below of testing whether or not your fabric is 100% cotton.

The Flame Test

Pull a few threads from the fabric and hold them carefully over a flame. Polyester and other synthetic fabrics will give off black smoke and the faint smell of plastic. Burning cotton smells like burning paper.

The Crease Test

Press a crease into the fabric with your fingers. All-cotton fabric creases more easily than polyester or blends.

Fabric Grain

Fabric is woven with threads that run along the length and width. The direction of the threads is called the grain. All pieces for projects in this book are cut along the grain of the fabric unless there is a specific instruction otherwise.

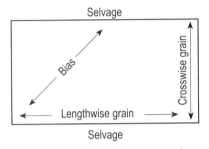

The lengthwise grain of the fabric is the least stretchy dimension. The crosswise grain stretches a little, more than the lengthwise grain. Cutting pieces for your projects along the grain ensures that they will maintain their shape as you handle them. Notice the arrows on each pattern piece. Line up arrows along the straight grain of fabric, either the lengthwise or crosswise grain.

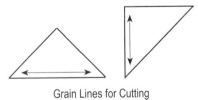

Grain Lines for Cutting

Cutting on the diagonal is known as cutting on the bias. The bias has a considerable amount of give and elasticity. Nearly all of the pattern pieces for these projects are cut on the straight grain, but you will cut binding on the bias since binding needs elasticity. Pay close attention to the direction your pattern pieces are cut as this is one of the keys to successful patchwork.

Be sure to press your fabric in preparation for cutting. I recommend a steam iron to get rid of all wrinkles.

Rotary Cutting

All the projects in this book can be cut using a rotary cutter except for a few appliqué pieces that require templates. Rotary cutting is much faster and more accurate than template cutting.

Rotary cutters have revolutionized quiltmaking. They are the most accurate tools available for cutting straight edges. I highly recommend using a rotary cutter, but I also recommend becoming proficient in its use before attempting to cut your patchwork pieces, because without practice, you could cut yourself or ruin your fabric. If necessary, check with your fabric store or quilt shop and ask about classes in how to use a rotary cutter.

Rotary-cutter blades are easy to replace when they become dull. Replace your blade when it no longer cuts cleanly and easily through several layers of fabric. Keep extra blades on hand to prevent the frustration of cutting with a dull or nicked blade.

Each time you start a project, be sure to clean your cutter. Take the cutter apart and wipe the blade with a soft cloth. Reassemble the cutter and oil the blade by placing a drop of sewing machine oil on it. Run the blade across your cutting mat to spread the oil.

The one drawback of the rotary cutter is the ease with which you can cut yourself. If you are careful, accidents can be avoided. For safe rotary-cutter use, be sure you always cut away from your body, and before cutting, visually check the path the blade will take, making sure your fingers are not in the way!

A rotary cutter can easily cut through sixteen layers of fabric. If you are a beginning quilter, I suggest that you cut no more than four layers at a time. Also, remember that it is easier to cut shorter lengths of fabric than very long ones.

1. Lay the fabric on the mat, with the folded edge toward you and selvages away from you. Line up the folded fabric edge on the lowest solid horizontal line.

Align the fabric so that the left raw edge extends slightly beyond a solid inch line on the mat grid.

2. To cut off the ragged edges and make a clean, crisp line on the left side of your fabric as a starting point, set the ruler over the fabric on the left side (on the right side if you are left-handed). Align the ruler with the nearest solid vertical line.

3. Set one side of the Bias Square on the bottom fold of fabric and adjust the long ruler so that it is also flush with the Bias Square. With one hand, press firmly on the ruler to hold it in place and with the other hand, use the rotary cutter to cut through the fabric from the fold to the top edge.

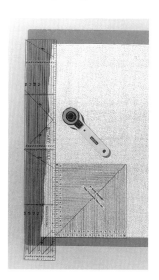
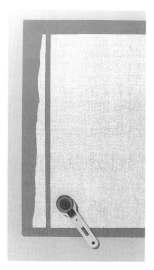

The projects in this book require you to make several basic types of cuts. You will cut strips, which are then crosscut into squares or rectangles. Some squares are cut on the diagonal to create half-square triangles. In some quilt plans, squares are cut first on one diagonal, then the other, to create quarter-square triangles. Finally, there are pieces that must be traced onto the fabric using a template and cut with scissors. See "Using Templates" on page 11.

Cutting Strips

To cut a 3" x 3" square, first cut a strip that is 3" wide. Set the Bias Square to the right of the ruler on the fold of the fabric as before, and with the 3" line on your long ruler aligned with the edge of the fabric, make the cut.

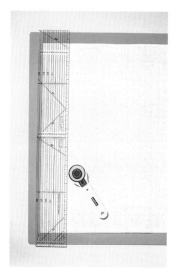

Cutting Squares and Rectangles

Set the extra fabric aside and concentrate on the 3" strip just cut. Now, making sure the strip is carefully aligned horizontally along a solid grid line on the cutting mat, set the bottom edge of the Bias Square along the bottom edge of the strip and trim away the selvage edges of the strip. Then, move the Bias Square to the correct position to cut a 3" square and make crosscuts, working from left to right. Don't forget to check the alignment of the Bias Square before each individual cut.

If you are cutting rectangles, follow the same procedure but make the second cut the length of your rectangle.

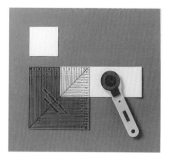

Cutting Half-Square Triangles

Cut squares in half diagonally to create triangles with the straight grain on the two short sides. To account for seam allowances, cut squares ⅞" larger than the desired finished size of the pieced square.

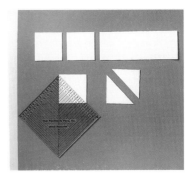

Cutting Quarter-Square Triangles

Cut a square twice diagonally. The resulting triangles have the straight grain on their longest edges. To account for seam allowances, cut squares 1¼" larger than the desired finished size of the pieced square.

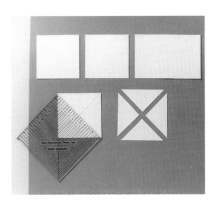

Most of the quilt patterns in this book require either half-square or quarter-square triangles. All are cut as shown above. The cutting instructions for each pattern list the size and number of squares to cut.

Using Templates

If you prepare and store your patterns neatly, using the tips that follow, they will serve you well and accurately in your appliqué, patchwork, and sewing projects.

I recommend photocopying or tracing the templates and patterns to preserve the book. Photocopy the templates on card stock or heavy paper, or trace the templates onto template plastic (available at most quilt stores). Be sure to go to a high-quality copy shop because low-quality machines tend to distort lines and can ruin the accuracy of your project.

To hold paper templates and patterns and keep them organized, glue a large manila envelope to the inside back cover of this book. Then, you have a complete and accurate set available whenever you want to use or reuse them.

The templates for the projects in this book include seam allowances. To cut shapes using a template, trace the template shapes onto template plastic, using a sharp pencil. Be sure to trace grain-line arrows, too. Cut out the template shapes carefully with sharp scissors. Place a template on the fabric, orienting it according to the grain-line arrows, and use one of the following techniques.

- Trace around the template onto the wrong side of the fabric, using either a pencil or a water-soluble marking pen. Cut on the marked line with scissors.
- Press your hand on the template to steady it as you rotary cut along its edge.

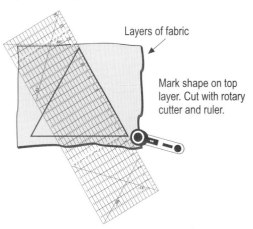

Layers of fabric

Mark shape on top layer. Cut with rotary cutter and ruler.

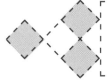

Patchwork Tips

Accuracy is of the utmost importance in patchwork, and precise cutting is at the heart of that accuracy. It requires special care in preparing the fabric, in marking the shapes onto the fabric with templates, and in the actual cutting. These tips will help make your quiltmaking more accurate and easier to do.

Iron Before Cutting

Before cutting out shapes, press the fabric with a hot steam iron. Wrinkles or folds in the fabric will cause distortions in fabric shapes.

Cut on the Straight of Grain

Cut shapes so that their straight edges are on the lengthwise or crosswise grain of the fabric, unless specifically directed to do otherwise. Pieces cut on the bias (diagonal) of the fabric will have extra elasticity and may not fit the edges of the other patchwork pieces smoothly and accurately.

Glue Sandpaper to Templates

Gluing a piece of sandpaper to the back of a paper or plastic template, with the gritty side facing down, is a great trick for cutting accurate shapes from fabric. The sandpaper adds weight and sturdiness to the template, and the rough surface grips the fabric for a more accurate cut. *Do not cut sandpaper with your fabric scissors!*

Perfectly cut fabric shapes alone will not make a successful project. They must be sewn together with care and accuracy.

Mark and Pin Seam Intersections

Whichever cutting method you choose, mark fabric at the seam intersections. For paper or plastic templates, take a large, sharp needle (or $3/16$" hole punch) and puncture templates at the points where seams cross. Mark those on the fabric pieces with a removable marking pen.

For rotary-cut pieces, use a quilter's ruler and mark the points where the seams intersect. Before stitching two pieces of fabric together, put a pin through the marked seam intersection on the first piece of fabric and then through the corresponding spot on the other piece of fabric. Secure the pin after you are sure that the points line up exactly.

Check Your Stitch Length

Set your sewing machine for short, straight stitches, about 12 per inch. Long, loose stitches can come undone. Small stitches add strength to the patchwork.

Backstitch

Stitch back and forth a short distance at both ends of each seam, to prevent it from coming undone.

Stitch Uniform Seams

All of the patchwork projects in this book require 1/4"-wide seam allowances. Variations will distort the shape of the project, and the seams will not meet as they should. If your sewing machine doesn't have a stitching guide, you can place a piece of tape exactly 1/4" from the needle to use as a guide.

Press Seam Allowances Toward the Darker Fabric

After stitching together individual pieces, strips, or blocks, press seam allowances toward the darker fabric whenever possible. Pressing the seam allowances this way prevents darker seam allowances from showing through lighter color fabrics on the front of the project.

Press Seam Allowances in Opposite Directions

When you sew together rows or pairs of pieces, press the seam allowances of one row or pair in one direction and the seam allowances of the other row or pair in the opposite direction. When you pin the rows into place, the seam allowances butt up against each other in what I call the "natural groove," and this gives the joined seams a firmer fit.

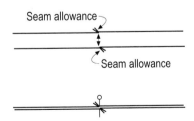

Hand Appliqué

There are several methods of hand appliqué that give good results. My preferred method requires a paper sewing-line template for each appliqué piece.

1. Using a template that includes the seam allowance, cut out the appliqué shapes from your fabric.

 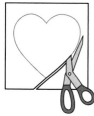

2. Make a paper template without the seam allowance for each appliqué shape. Center the template on the wrong side of the fabric shape and fold the seam allowance of the fabric smoothly over the edges to the back of the paper.

3. Baste completely around the fabric shape, sewing through the paper and the fabric. Clip sharp inside curves almost to the seam line.

4. Using a glue stick, spread glue on the paper template and attach the fabric shape to the right side of the background fabric, being careful to place it in the exact spot desired. Press it with a warm iron to secure.

5. Appliqué the shape to the background fabric, using small stitches that catch only two or three threads at the edge of the appliqué piece.

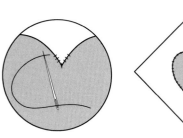 

Embroidery Stitches

The two embroidery stitches below are the only ones you will need for the projects in this book. Use three strands of embroidery thread to make these stitches.

Backstitch

Bring the needle through the fabric from back to front (A). Put the needle tip through the fabric about $\frac{1}{8}$" to the right (B) and bring it back up about $\frac{1}{8}$" to the left of the starting point (C). For the next stitch, push the needle into the fabric at the starting point (A) and bring it out $\frac{1}{8}$" to the left of the exit point for the first stitch (C). Continue, forming a smooth outline stitch.

French Knot

Bring the needle through the fabric from back to front. Wind the floss around the needle two or three times and push the needle back through the fabric close to where it first came out. Holding the knot against the fabric, pull the thread through to the back, leaving the knot on top.

Backstitch   French Knot

Making Prairie Points

Prairie points add a special decorative touch to the edges of a quilt. The color and shape of the points can provide emphasis and interest to your design. Squares of fabric are folded into triangles that are then overlapped and pinned together into a chain. They are stitched to the edge of a quilt instead of binding.

Twelve 3" x 3" squares of fabric folded into prairie points and set just inside one another make approximately 20" of edging. The points can be set more or less deeply into each other for varying lengths and for different effects. Experiment by pinning together several prairie points and measure the length of the edging created.

1. Cut squares of fabric, each $3\frac{1}{2}$" x $3\frac{1}{2}$".

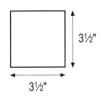

2. Fold each square once on the diagonal. Fold again on the other diagonal. Press the folded squares with a hot iron.

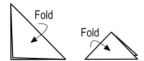

3. Measure the sides of the quilt. Pin the edge of a prairie point just inside another prairie point as shown. Repeat to make a chain of prairie points as long as required for each side of the quilt.

4. Pin the cut edge of a chain of prairie points to the front side of the quilt. Adjust as necessary, so that prairie points meet as shown in the corners. Stitch, using a $\frac{1}{4}$"-wide seam allowance. Repeat for each side.

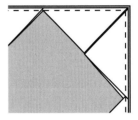

Applying Piping

Follow these easy steps to apply ready-made piping to pillows, tote bags, or quilts.

1. Measure and cut the finished length of the piping you need plus $\frac{1}{2}$". Remove 1" of piping stitching. Pull back the fabric that covers the cording. Trim the cording inside to the exact finished length you need.

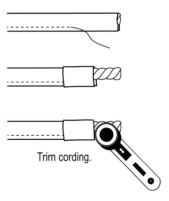

Trim cording.

2. Fold the piping cover fabric under so that it ends exactly where the cording ends.

Fold ends under.

3. Restitch the piping fabric together all the way to the end.

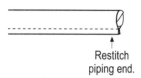

Restitch piping end.

4. Prepare each piping end using this method, so that there are no raw edges where the ends meet. Join the ends together and stitch by hand around the edges of the piping cover fabric to finish the piped edging.

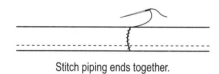

Stitch piping ends together.

Preparing Batting

You can purchase batting in two forms: presized batting or batting by the yard that can be cut to the desired length. Batting on a roll is often 60" wide and is usually less expensive than precut batting. But, for large quilts, buying a presized batting is easier because batting by the yard requires piecing to make it large enough for full-size quilts. The quilts in this book are small enough that you will not need to piece your batting.

Cut the batting a few inches larger than the quilt top. During the quilting process, the batting edges can fray. It is best to have a little extra so you can trim the batting with the backing to a neat, straight edge when you are ready to quilt.

Batting comes in various weights, but I prefer the lightest-weight batting, especially for beginners, as it is the easiest to quilt through. If you try to quilt through a heavy batting when you quilt your first project, you are likely to become discouraged and miss out on the joy of hand quilting.

Backing

All of the projects in this book are small enough that the backing can be made from one width of fabric without piecing. However, you may want to be creative and piece or appliqué designs on your quilt backing just for fun. I recommend that you embroider the quilt's name, your name, and the date the quilt was finished on a small piece of fabric and then appliqué it somewhere on the back of the quilt so it can be identified by anyone interested in the quilt's origin.

Be sure to cut the fabric for the backing approximately 2" larger than the quilt top on all four sides. Quilting often shrinks the quilt slightly, and this extra fabric ensures that the backing will be large enough.

Basting

Basting is not one of my favorite parts of the quiltmaking process. It is time-consuming, but it ensures that your quilt will lie smooth and flat. When I have not taken the time to baste correctly, I have been disappointed with the result: a quilt with puckers or twists. There are two methods of basting that I recommend: with a needle and thread or with safety pins.

Needle and Thread

Use a regular sewing needle and bright contrasting thread. Beginning at the center of the quilt, use long running stitches to baste the layers together in horizontal rows about 6" to 8" apart, then stitch in vertical rows until the whole quilt is basted and all fabric lies flat. Do not remove the basting until the entire project is quilted.

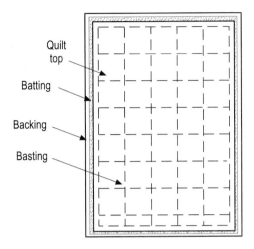

Quilt top
Batting
Backing
Basting

Safety Pins

This is a fast and easy way of basting. Using small safety pins, begin pinning your quilt from the center out. Push the first pin through the three layers in the center of the quilt, then working in rows, fasten a pin through the quilt every few inches until the quilt is completely pinned and ready for quilting. I like this method because you can remove pins as you quilt.

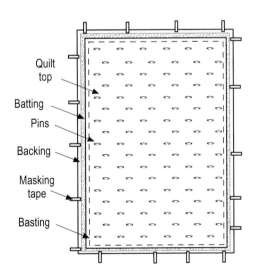

Quilt top
Batting
Pins
Backing
Masking tape
Basting

Quilting

Quilting is usually a three-step process: marking the quilt top, basting the layers together, then quilting.

Marking the top in preparation for quilting is important since the lines you mark are your quilting guides. The outline quilting and other straight quilting lines suggested in the quilt plans do not need to be marked. You can use $1/4$"-wide quilter's tape and quilt along its edge. The motif quilting designs in the "Needles and Spools" and the "Ninepatch Sampler" quilts must be marked.

For marking small quilts and wall hangings, I recommend two techniques: the light box or the window.

Light Box

A light box is often used by photographers and is a most helpful marking tool. Simply place the design on the box with the light turned on. Set the quilt top over the design at the desired point and trace the design with a quilt marking pen onto the quilt top.

You can create a makeshift light box by pulling apart your dining table, as if to insert a leaf, and placing a piece of glass or Plexiglas over the gap. A lighted lamp on the floor beneath the table provides the light.

Make your own "light box."

Window

Find a window in your house with lots of glass uninterrupted by panes. Tape the quilting motif to the window. Tape the quilt top over the motif in the desired location, mark with a removable marking pen, move the quilt to the next spot for marking, and tape it up again. The light behind the window illuminates the motif and makes it easy to trace.

For large quilts, some quilters use a quilting frame, pinning the quilt to fabric that has been nailed to the frame's edges. For the small quilts in this book, use a quilting hoop. A quilting hoop is heavier than an embroidery hoop. The quilting hoop may come with an attached stand and may be made of wood or plastic.

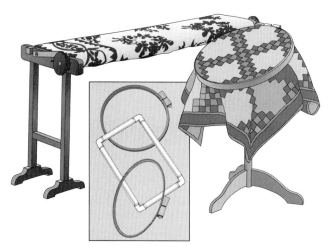

Quilting consists of short running stitches, usually through two layers of fabric and one of batting. Many people believe that tied coverlets may be classified as quilts as long as they include patchwork, but tied coverlets are actually comforters. Only pieces with running stitches binding the layers together qualify as true quilts.

To quilt by hand:
1. Thread the needle with an 18"-long strand of quilting thread. Make a small knot in one end.
2. Push the needle through the quilt top about 1" from where your quilting line will begin. Push the needle out at the point where the stitching will be and gently pull the thread until the knot pops through the fabric and into the batting.
3. Take small, even stitches through all three layers, rocking the needle up and down and taking three or more stitches on the needle at a time.

4. To end a line of quilting, make a small knot close to the last stitch, then take a backstitch through the quilt top and bring the needle up a needle's length away. Pull the thread until the knot pops into the batting and carefully clip the thread at the surface of the quilt.

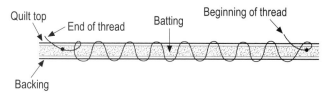

All of the projects in this book were quilted by hand. Complete quilting diagrams are provided. You may follow the patterns or design your own. The following defines the major quilting styles.
- *Single Outline Quilting* follows the seam lines of the patchwork pieces, with stitching ¼" away from the seam.
- *Double Outline Quilting* consists of two lines of stitching that follow the seam lines. The first line is ¼" from the seam, the second is ¼" from the first line.
- *Quilting in-the-Ditch* is stitching as close to the seam as possible on the side with no seam allowance underneath.
- *Motif Quilting* involves quilting a design from the simple to the ornate, usually in an unpieced area, such as a border or the center of a block.

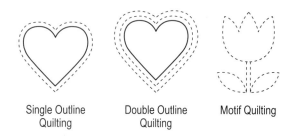

Single Outline Quilting   Double Outline Quilting   Motif Quilting

Making Bias Binding

When the quilting is finished, trim the batting and backing to the same size as the quilt top in preparation for binding.

All but one of the quilts in this book require binding. Bias binding is cut on the bias, or the diagonal, of the fabric. You may use bias quilting tape that comes precut and packaged, or you may make your own binding. Buying the binding is quick and easy. Making your own binding lets you match your quilt exactly.

I used either a ¼ yard or ⅓ yard piece of fabric to make bias binding for the quilts in this book. The smaller the piece of fabric, the shorter the bias strips. Follow these steps to make bias binding:

1. Trim away the fabric selvages and cut 2"-wide strips on the bias of the fabric.
2. To stitch the strips together end to end, trim the ends of the strips to a 45° angle and place them right sides together as shown. Sew them together and press the seams open.

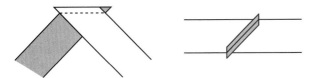

3. Piece as necessary to make bias strips for each side of the quilt. Make each strip 4" longer than the side of the quilt. Stitch strips to two opposite sides of the quilt with 2" extending on each end as shown.

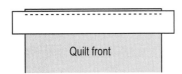

Fold the binding to the back of the quilt, turn the binding under ¼", and slipstitch to finish the edge. Trim away the excess binding.

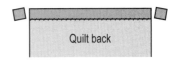

4. Stitch a binding strip to each of the remaining sides with 2" extending at each end.
5. Trim the ends to ¼" beyond the ends of the quilt.

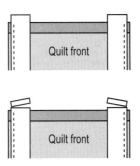

6. Open the binding and fold the ¼"-wide seam allowances at the corners to the back. Fold under a ¼"-wide seam allowance along the edge of the binding strip and blindstitch the binding to the back of the quilt.

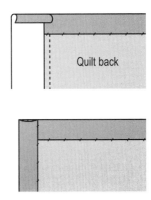

Adding a Sleeve

Once your small quilt is completed, you may want to hang it on the wall. The best way to do so and still protect the shape of your quilt is to make a hanging sleeve for the back so you can slip a dowel through it. The dowel supports the quilt all along the top rather than at just one or two points.

1. Cut a strip of fabric 8" wide and ½" shorter than the completed width of your quilt.
2. Turn the strip under ¼" at both ends. Press with a hot iron, turn under ¼" again, and stitch by machine to finish the ends.
3. Now fold your strip in half lengthwise, wrong sides together, with raw edges aligned. Stitch along the length of the strip ¼" from the raw edges.

Hem ends, then seam raw edges, right side out.

4. Open the seam, center it on the tube shape you have created, and press.

Center seam and press open.

5. Pin the tube in place just below the top inner edge of the binding. Blindstitch the top edge of the tube sleeve to your quilt. Be sure your stitches do not go through to the front side of the quilt.

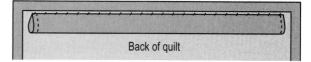

Back of quilt

Tack down top edge of sleeve.

6. Push the tube up just a little before sewing the other edge to the quilt. This will give a little fullness so the dowel will have enough room to slide comfortably through the sleeve.

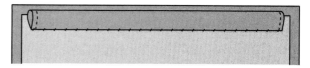

Push tube up and tack down bottom edge.

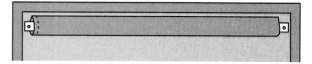

Insert hanging rod in sleeve.

Making a Pillow

Making a pillow is an easy introduction to working with patchwork and quilting. Choose one of the twenty-one block patterns in this book or any pattern of your choice. A good, basic size for a pillow is 12" x 12"; however, a pillow can be any size you want it to be. I recently bought a pillow at a quilt show that was made from a scrap of an antique quilt, and it measured just 3" x 6".

Most of the blocks in this book are not 12" x 12"; they are smaller. You can easily enlarge the size of a block by adding strips of fabric around the edges. Do some designing by drawing your pillow top on graph paper. Draw the shape you want your pillow to be, and calculate the width and length of the strips you need to add. Add ½" for seam allowances when you cut the strips.

A few of the patchwork designs need special treatment, such as the Wild Goose Chase and Fish blocks. The Wild Goose Chase block is only 3" x 3". You could make three rows of three Wild Goose Chase blocks for a 9" x 9" square pillow. The Fish block is 6" x 9". Sew four together to form a 12" x 18" shape. Strips can be added to enlarge any shape.

For example, follow these steps to make a 12" x 12" pillow from the 8" x 8" Pinwheel pattern.

1. Add a 2½" x 8½" strip to each side of the Pinwheel block.
2. Add a 2½" x 12½" strip to the top and bottom edges.

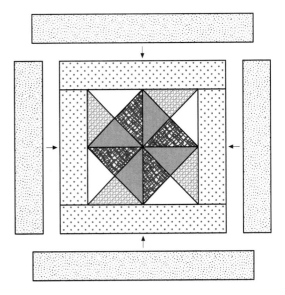

3. Cut a block of lightweight batting slightly larger than your pillow top. Use small safety pins to attach the top and the batting.
4. Quilt the piece as the diagram suggests or create a quilting design of your own!

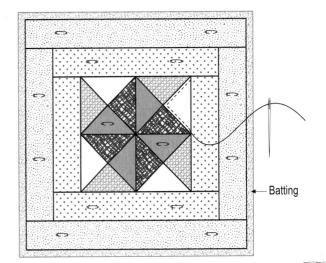

Batting

5. Remove the safety pins and decide how you are going to edge the pillow. There are several choices to consider: lace, piping, braid, or prairie points. You can also just leave the edges plain.

6. Sew the desired edging to the front of the quilted pillow top ¼" from the edge.

7. Cut a backing for your pillow the same size as the top.

8. Place the top and back right sides together and sew around the edges, leaving a 3" opening between the beginning and end of the stitching.

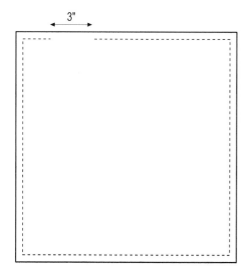

9. Turn the pillow right side out through the opening and stuff it with fiberfill. Be sure to push filling into the corners. (Use a large knitting needle if necessary.)

10. Close the opening along the seam with small, invisible stitches.

Making a Tote Bag

Another way to use your patchwork blocks is to make a tote bag. Follow steps 1–4 for making a pillow top. You may want a bag that is larger than a 12" x 12" pillow, so add the strips necessary to obtain the block size you desire. In the following instructions, the finished bag size is 16" x 16".

1. Cut 3 squares of fabric, each 16½" x 16½", for the back and lining. Cut 2 squares of batting, each 16½" x 16½".
2. Layer the batting with the tote bag top. Quilt, following the diagram on page 51, or make up your own quilting design.

3. Place the back and front right sides together and stitch them together from the top, right side down, then across the bottom edge and up the left side.
4. Press the top edge under ¼" toward the wrong side and turn the bag right side out.

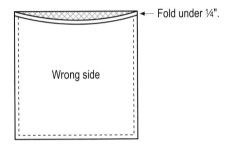

5. Cut fabric for the inner pocket 6½" x 8½".
6. Press the top edge under ¼" toward the wrong side of the fabric. Press under ¼" again and stitch along the folded edge to finish.

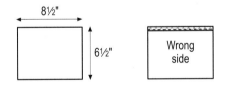

Patchwork bag front
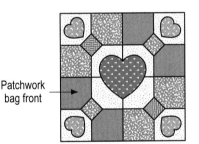

Outer back

Lining front

Lining back

7. Center the pocket vertically and horizontally on the right side of the back lining and stitch down the right side, across the bottom, and up the left side. Stitch through the center of the pocket to make two sections. Backstitch at the top to make the seam stronger.

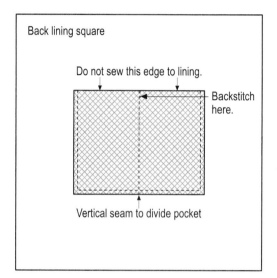

Back lining square

Do not sew this edge to lining.

Backstitch here.

Vertical seam to divide pocket

Now place the linings right sides together and stitch them together as you did for the front and back: down the right side, across the bottom edge, and up the left side. Do not turn linings right side out. Press the top edge ¼" under toward the wrong side.

Turn edge down ¼" and press.

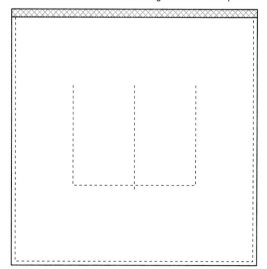

8. Cut 2 strips of fabric, each 1½" by 15½", for the handles.

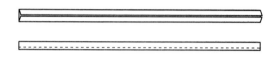

15½"

1½"

9. Fold the edges of the strips to the center. Then fold the strip in half and stitch along the edge.

10. Stitch the handles in place at the top of the bag in the front and back.

11. Place the lining inside the bag and insert the second square of batting between the back of the bag and the back of the lining. Then sew the top edges of the bag and lining together, using small stitches.

Insert batting between bag and lining.

Stitch lining and bag together around top.

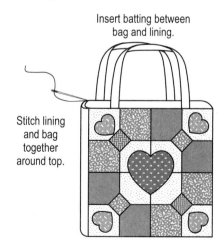

The Gallery

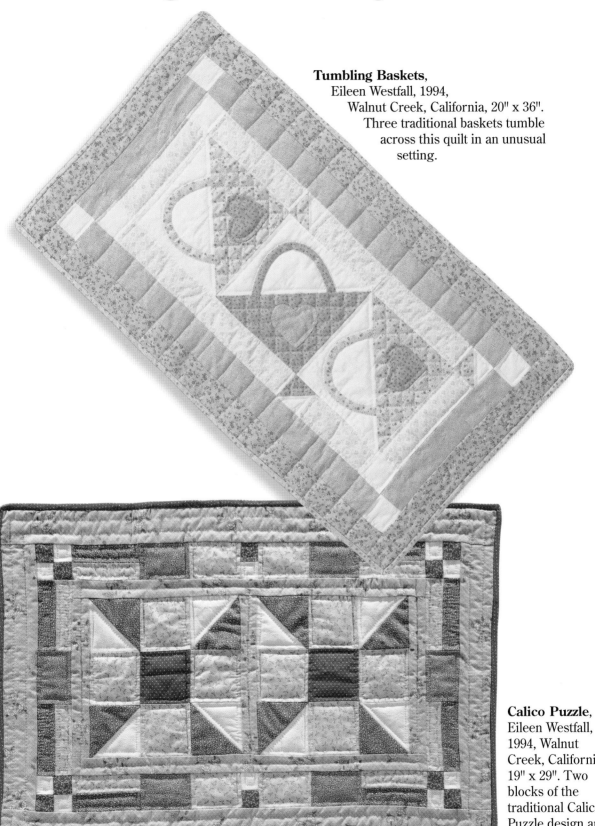

Tumbling Baskets,
Eileen Westfall, 1994,
Walnut Creek, California, 20" x 36".
Three traditional baskets tumble
across this quilt in an unusual
setting.

Calico Puzzle,
Eileen Westfall,
1994, Walnut
Creek, California,
19" x 29". Two
blocks of the
traditional Calico
Puzzle design are
set side by side.

Grandmother's Rainbow Fan, Eileen Westfall, 1994, Walnut Creek, California, 40" x 40". I love rainbows, so I decided to create a rainbow look using a fan pattern. The twist was to put four fans in different positions on a black background rather than the usual white.

Pinwheels and Posies, Eileen Westfall, 1993, Walnut Creek, California, 28" x 28". Two Flower blocks and two Pinwheel blocks form the center of this quilt.

Hearts and Bow Ties, Eileen Westfall, 1994, Walnut Creek, California, 20" x 20". The Bow Tie block gets a little added style with appliquéd hearts.

27

Ninepatch Sampler, Eileen Westfall, 1994, Walnut Creek, California, 39" x 39". There are four classic blocks in this piece: Ohio Star, Clown's Choice, Box Kite, and Churn Dash.

Four Log Cabins, Eileen Westfall, 1994, Walnut Creek, California, 26" x 26". The classic Log Cabin pattern is paired with an original Cabin block. Mini–Log Cabin corners border the patchwork.

Sailboat and Fish, Eileen Westfall, 1994, Walnut Creek, California, 30" x 30". A simple Sailboat block in the center and pieced fish borders complete the look of this maritime piece.

Leaves of the Season, Eileen Westfall, 1994, Walnut Creek, California, 27" x 27". These fall leaves, in shades of green to brown, were easy to piece, using squares and half-square triangle units.

Stars and Stripes, Eileen Westfall, 1993, Walnut Creek, California, 24" x 24". The easiest of all the quilts in this book, this design combines simple pieced red stars and blue stripes to form the block.

Needles and Spools, Eileen Westfall, 1994, Walnut Creek, California, 27" x 45". The Spools pattern is a popular classic. I decided to add embroidered needles and thread tails to enhance the design. The Wild Goose Chase border is a favorite of mine.

Londontown Roads, Eileen Westfall, 1994, Walnut Creek, California, 20" x 20". Some years ago, I saw a movie in which Diane Keaton had a beautiful quilt on her bed. I loved the pattern, which looked like arrows coming together. I found the design in an encyclopedia of patchwork patterns and decided to include it in this book.

The Projects

Calico Puzzle

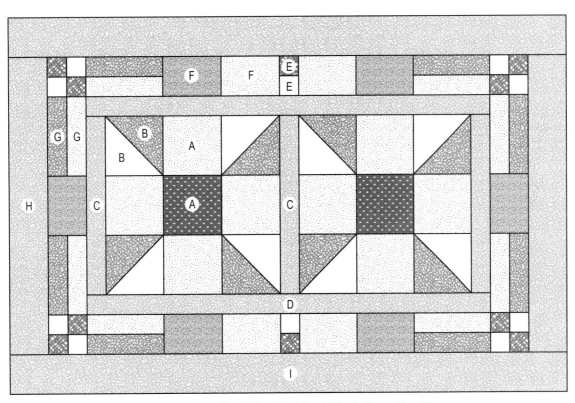

Quilt Size: 19" x 29" • Finished Block Size: 9" x 9"

Dark rust print #1   Medium rust print   Muslin   Light green print

Dark rust print #2   Cream print   Dark green print

Materials (44"-wide fabric)
$\frac{1}{8}$ yd. dark rust print #1
$\frac{1}{8}$ yd. dark rust print #2
$\frac{1}{8}$ yd. medium rust print
$\frac{1}{4}$ yd. cream print
$\frac{1}{4}$ yd. unbleached muslin
$\frac{1}{4}$ yd. dark green print
1 yd. light green print for borders and
   backing
21" x 31" piece of batting
$\frac{1}{3}$ yd. for binding

Cutting
From dark rust print #1, cut:
2 squares, each $3\frac{1}{2}$" x $3\frac{1}{2}$", for piece A

From dark rust print #2, cut:
10 squares, each $1\frac{1}{2}$" x $1\frac{1}{2}$", for piece E

From medium rust print, cut:
6 rectangles, each $2\frac{1}{2}$" x $3\frac{1}{2}$", for piece F

From cream print, cut:
8 squares, each 3½" x 3½", for piece A
4 rectangles, each 2½" x 3½", for piece F
8 rectangles, each 1½" x 4½", for
    piece G

From unbleached muslin, cut:
4 squares, each 3⅞" x 3⅞", cut once diago-
    nally for 8 piece B
10 squares, each 1½" x 1½", for piece E

From dark green print, cut:
4 squares, each 3⅞" x 3⅞", cut once diago-
    nally for 8 piece B
8 rectangles, each 1½" x 4½", for
    piece G

From light green print, cut:
3 strips, each 1½" x 9½", for piece C
2 strips, each 1½" x 21½", for piece D
2 strips, each 2½" x 15½", for piece H
2 strips, each 2½" x 29½", for piece I
1 square, 21" x 31", for backing

Block Assembly

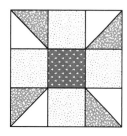
Calico Puzzle Block

1. To make half-square triangle units, sew
   a dark green piece B triangle to a muslin
   piece B triangle as shown, being careful
   not to stretch the bias edges. Press the
   seams toward the dark green triangles.

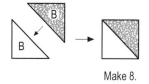
Make 8.

2. For each block, arrange 4 half-square
   triangle units with 4 cream piece A
   squares and 1 dark rust #1 piece A
   square in 3 rows of 3 as shown.

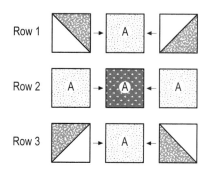

3. Sew the squares together in rows. Press
   the seams of Rows 1 and 3 in one direction and the seams of Row 2 in the
   opposite direction.

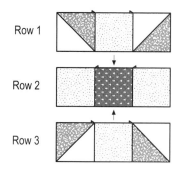

4. Sew the rows together to form the
   Calico Puzzle block.

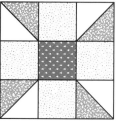
Make 2.

Quilt Top Assembly

1. Sew a Calico Puzzle block to each side of a light green piece C strip as shown.

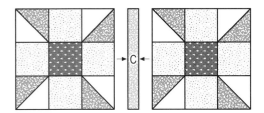

2. Sew a light green piece C strip to the outside edge of each Calico Puzzle block.

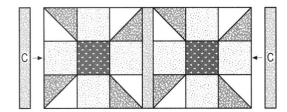

3. Sew a light green piece D strip to the top and bottom edges of the patchwork.

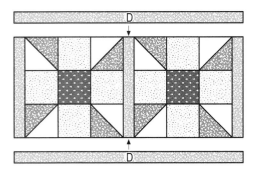

4. Sew a cream piece G rectangle to a dark green piece G rectangle.

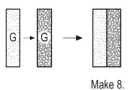

Make 8.

Note: The fabrics in the G/G units on the left side are the reverse of those on the right. This means that if you are using a directional fabric for either piece G, you must make two sets that mirror each other.

5. Arrange 4 of the G/G units with 2 medium rust piece F rectangles to make 2 side border strips as shown.

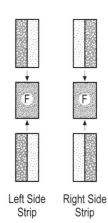

Left Side Strip   Right Side Strip

6. Sew the units together to form the 2 side borders. Press the seams toward the medium rust rectangles.

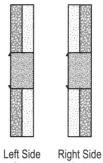

Left Side Strip   Right Side Strip

7. Sew the border strips to the sides of the patchwork as shown, paying careful attention to color placement. Press the seams toward the inner borders.

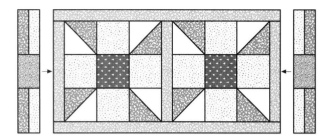

8. Sew a muslin piece E square to a dark rust #2 piece E square. Press the seam toward the dark rust squares in each unit.

Make 10.

9. Arrange the pieces as shown for top and bottom border strips. Sew the pieces together and press seams toward the darker fabric.

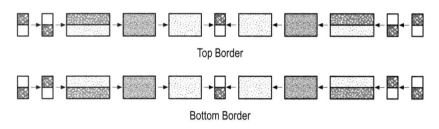

Top Border

Bottom Border

10. Add the top and bottom pieced borders to the quilt top, taking care to match the seams of the Four Patch corner blocks with the side border seams. Press the seams toward the center of the quilt.

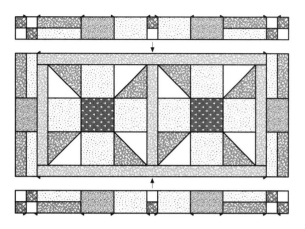

11. Sew a light green piece H strip to each side of the patchwork as shown. Press seams toward the outer border.

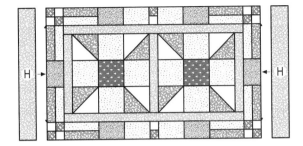

12. Sew light green piece I strips to the top and bottom edges of the patchwork. Press the seams toward the outer border.

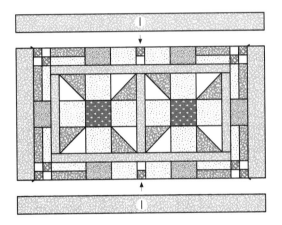

Finishing Touches

Refer to "Quilt Finishing Basics," beginning on page 15.

1. Layer the quilt top with batting and backing, and baste the layers together.
2. Quilt as shown in the diagram below or as desired.

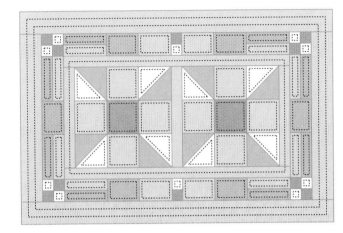

3. Bind the edges.
4. Add a hanging sleeve.

Four Log Cabins

Quilt Size: 26" x 26" • Finished Block Size: 10" x 10"

Materials (44"-wide fabric)
1/3 yd. purple paisley print
1/4 yd. dark purple print
1/8 yd. light green stripe
1/8 yd. medium green print
1/8 yd. dark green print #1
1/8 yd. dark green print #2
1/4 yd. white solid
Scraps of 4 dark purple prints
Scraps of 4 light purple prints
Scrap of light green check
7/8 yd. for backing
1/4 yd. for binding
28" x 28" square of batting

Cutting
Use Templates 1 and 2 on page 42.

From purple paisley, cut:
4 triangles, using Template 1, for piece A
4 rectangles, each 3" x 5 1/2", for piece M
4 rectangles, each 3" x 10 1/2", for piece N
2 rectangles, each 1 1/2" x 2 1/2", for piece J

From dark purple print, cut:
4 strips, each 3 1/2" x 20 1/2", for piece O

From light green striped fabric, cut:
2 rectangles, each 2 1/2" x 4 1/2", for
   piece C

4 rectangles, each 1½" x 3½", for piece D
4 squares, each 1½" x 1½", for piece I

From medium green print, cut:
4 rectangles, each 2½" x 5½", for piece F
4 rectangles, each 1½" x 2½", for piece J

From dark green print #1, cut:
2 rectangles, each 2½" x 3½", for
    piece E
4 squares, each 1½" x 1½", for piece I

From dark green print #2, cut:
4 rectangles, each 1½" x 2½", for piece J
2 rectangles, each 1½" x 8½", for
    piece H

From white solid, cut:
4 triangles, using Template 1, for piece A
2 rectangles, each 1½" x 8½", for
    piece H
4 rectangles, each 1½" x 10½", for
    piece G

From scraps of dark purple prints, cut:
2 chimney pieces, using Template 2, for
    piece B and piece B reversed
8 squares, each 1½" x 1½", for piece I
2 rectangles, each 1½" by 2½", for
    piece J
4 rectangles, each 1½" x 4½", for
    piece K

From scraps of light purple print, cut:
2 squares, each 1½" x 1½", for piece I
4 rectangles (2 each of 2 prints), each 1½" x
    3½", for piece D
2 rectangles, each 1½" x 5½", for
    piece L

From scrap of light green checked fabric, cut:
4 rectangles, each 1½" x 3½", for
    piece D

From the backing fabric, cut:
1 square, 28" x 28"

Cabin Block Assembly

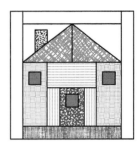

Cabin Block

Refer to "Hand Appliqué," beginning on page 14.

1. Appliqué piece B and piece B reversed to 2 white piece A triangles as shown.

2. Sew a purple paisley piece A triangle to make the roof/chimney units.

3. Sew a white piece A triangle to a purple paisley piece A triangle.

4. Sew the roof halves together to make 2 roof units.

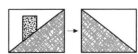

5. Sew a light green striped piece D rectangle to 2 sides of a dark green print #1 piece E rectangle, then sew a light

green striped piece C rectangle to the top edge to make the door unit.

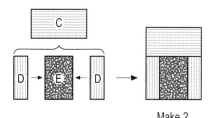

Make 2.

6. Sew medium green piece F rectangles to the sides of the door units, then sew a roof unit to the top of each door.

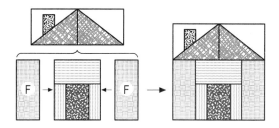

7. Sew a white piece H rectangle to the top edge of each cabin, and a dark green #2 piece H rectangle to the bottom edge of each.

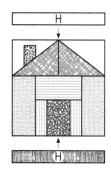

8. Sew white piece G rectangles to the sides of the Cabin blocks. Appliqué 3 dark purple piece I squares to each Cabin block to make windows.

Log Cabin Block Assembly

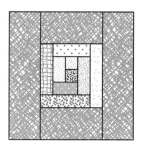

Log Cabin Block

1. Sew a light purple piece I square to a dark purple piece I square.

Make 2.

2. Sew a purple paisley piece J rectangle to the right sides of the units.

3. Sew a dark purple piece J rectangle to the top edge of the units.

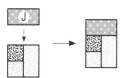

4. Sew a light purple piece D rectangle to the left side of the units.

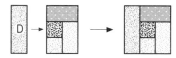

5. Sew a light purple piece D rectangle to the bottom edge of the units.

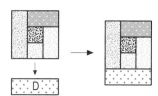

6. Sew a dark purple piece K rectangle to the right side of the units.

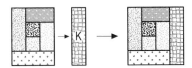

7. Sew a dark purple piece K rectangle to the top edge of the units.

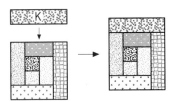

8. Sew a light purple piece L rectangle to the left side of the units.

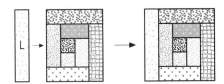

9. Sew a purple paisley piece M rectangle to the top and bottom edges of the blocks.

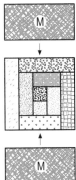

10. Sew a medium purple paisley piece N rectangle to each side of the Log Cabin blocks.

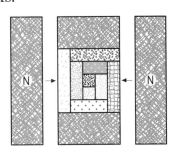

Quilt Top Assembly

1. Arrange the Cabin blocks and Log Cabin blocks as shown and sew them together in pairs. Press the seam in each pair toward the Log Cabin block.

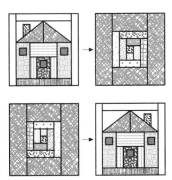

2. Sew the pairs together as shown, matching seams carefully.

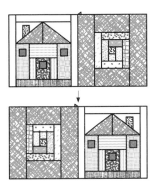

3. Sew a light green striped piece I square to a dark green #1 piece I square. Add a medium green piece J rectangle, a dark green print #2 piece J rectangle, and a light green checked piece D rectangle in order as shown to make 4 green print mini–Log Cabin blocks. After adding each piece, press the seam away from the center.

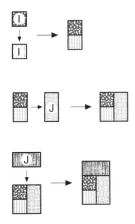

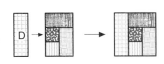

4. Sew a dark purple piece O strip to the sides of the quilt top. Press the seams toward the border.

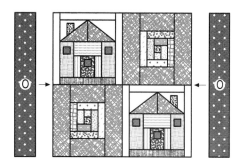

5. Sew a mini–Log Cabin block to each end of 2 dark purple O strips for the top and bottom borders. Be sure to consult the quilt plan or photo for color placement of the mini–Log Cabin blocks. Press seams toward the border.

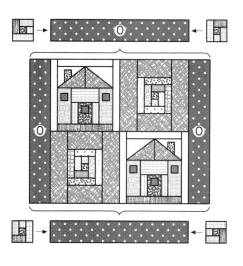

6. Sew the pieced outer border strips to the top and bottom of the quilt. Press seams toward the border.

Finishing Touches

Refer to "Quilt Finishing Basics," beginning on page 15.

1. Layer the quilt top with batting and backing, and baste the layers together.
2. Quilt as shown in the diagram below or as desired.

3. Bind the edges.
4. Add a hanging sleeve.

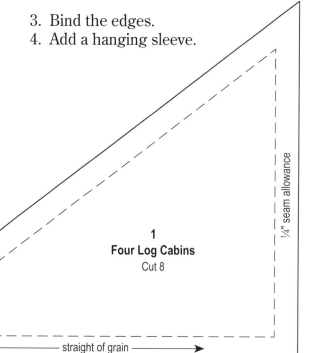

2
Four Log Cabins
Cut 1 and
1 reversed

Roof line

¼" seam allowance

1
Four Log Cabins
Cut 8

straight of grain

Grandmother's Rainbow Fan

Quilt Size: 40" x 40" • Finished Block Size: 12" x 12"

Purple print   Green print   Orange print   Black-and-white print #1

Blue print   Yellow print   Red pindot   Black-and-white print #2

Materials (44"-wide fabric)

¼ yd. purple print
¼ yd. blue print
¼ yd. green print
⅜ yd. yellow print
⅜ yd. orange print
2 yds. red pindot for blocks, backing, and
    binding
¾ yd. black-and-white print #1
¼ yd. black-and-white print #2
42" x 42" square of batting

Cutting

Use the fan-blade template on page 47.

From purple print, cut:
4 fan segments, using the template for
    piece A
2 squares, each 6¼" x 6¼", cut twice diago-
    nally for 8 piece C

From blue print, cut:
4 fan segments, using the template for
    piece A
2 squares, each 6¼" x 6¼", cut twice diago-
    nally for 8 piece C

From green print, cut:
4 fan segments, using the fan-blade template for piece A
2 squares, each 6¼" x 6¼", cut twice diagonally for 8 piece C
4 rectangles, each 3½" x 5½", for piece F

From yellow print, cut:
4 fan segments, using the template for piece A
2 squares, each 6¼" x 6¼", cut twice diagonally for 8 piece C
8 rectangles, each 3½" x 5½", for piece F

From orange print, cut:
4 fan segments, using the template for piece A
8 rectangles, each 3½" x 5½", for piece F

From red pindot, cut:
4 fan segments, using the template for piece A
2 rectangles, each 2" x 5½", for piece D
2 rectangles, each 2" x 8½", for piece E
8 rectangles, each 3½" x 5½", for piece F

From black-and-white print #1, cut:
4 squares, each 12½" x 12½", for piece B
8 rectangles, each 2" x 5½", for piece D
6 strips, each 2" x 24½", for piece G

From black-and-white print #2, cut:
8 rectangles, each 2" x 5½", for piece D
8 rectangles, each 2" x 8½", for piece E

From the backing fabric, cut:
1 square, 42" x 42".

Block Assembly

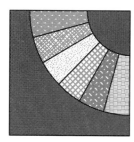

Rainbow Fan Block

1. Arrange the A pieces into 2 pairs of rainbow fans as shown. Notice that the color placement in one pair is the mirror image of the other pair.

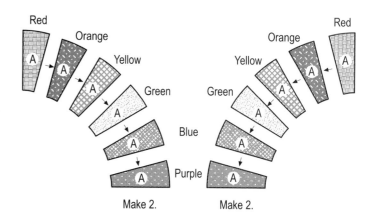

Make 2.   Make 2.

2. Sew the fan pieces together. Press seams toward the bottom edge of fan.

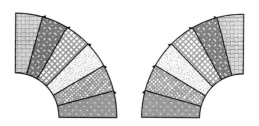

3. Referring to "Hand Appliqué," beginning on page 14, appliqué the fans to black-and-white #1 piece B squares.

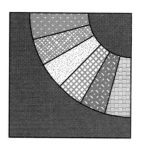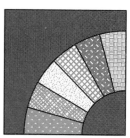

Make 2.   Make 2.

4. Arrange the Fan blocks as shown and sew them together in pairs. Press the seam between one pair in one direction and the seam between the other pair in

the opposite direction. Then sew the pairs together.

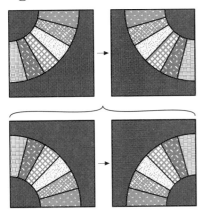

Corner and Center Block Assembly

1. Arrange 5 sets of piece C triangles to form squares. Sew pairs of triangles together. Press seams in opposite directions.

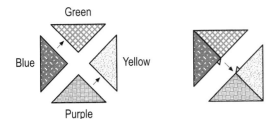

2. Sew the triangle units together, matching seams, to form squares.

Make 5.

3. Sew 2 piece D rectangles and 2 piece E rectangles of red pindot to the sides and top and bottom of 1 square, as shown, for the center block.

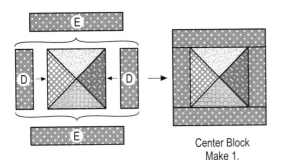

Center Block
Make 1.

4. Sew 2 black-and-white #2 piece D rectangles to the sides and 2 black-and-white #2 piece E rectangles to the top and bottom of 4 squares as shown for the corner blocks. Set aside.

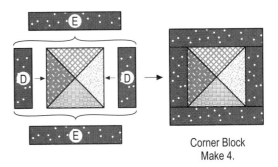

Corner Block
Make 4.

5. Referring to "Hand Appliqué," beginning on page 14, appliqué the center block made in step 3 to the center of the quilt top.

Pieced Border Assembly

1. Arrange the F rectangles into 4 strips as shown.

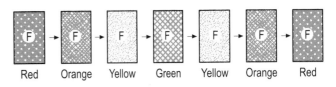

Red   Orange   Yellow   Green   Yellow   Orange   Red

2. Sew the rectangles together into 4 border strips. Press the seams toward the darker fabrics.

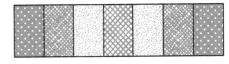

Make 4.

3. Sew a black-and-white #1 piece D rectangle to the ends of each of the 4 border strips. Press the seam toward the piece D rectangles.

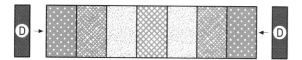

4. Sew a black-and-white #1 piece G strip to the long sides of the 4 border strips. Press the seams toward piece G.

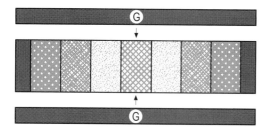

5. Sew 1 of the pieced border strips to the top and bottom of the quilt top as shown. Press the seams toward the border.

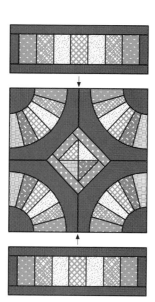

6. Sew a corner block to the top and bottom of each of the 2 remaining border strips as shown. Press the seams toward the corner blocks.

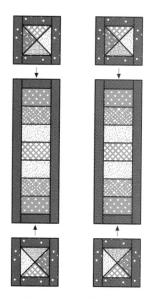

Left Border   Right Border

7. Add the side borders to the quilt top, matching the seams of the corner blocks with the seams of the top and bottom borders. Press the seams toward the borders.

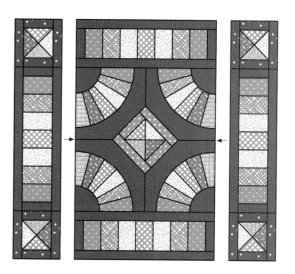

Finishing Touches

Refer to "Quilt Finishing Basics," beginning on page 15.

1. Layer the quilt top with batting and backing, and baste the layers together.

2. Quilt as shown in the diagram below or as desired.
3. Bind the edges.
4. Add a hanging sleeve.

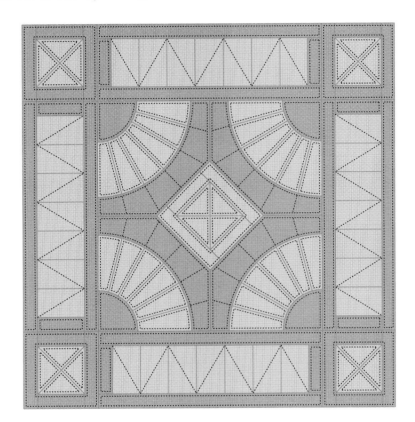

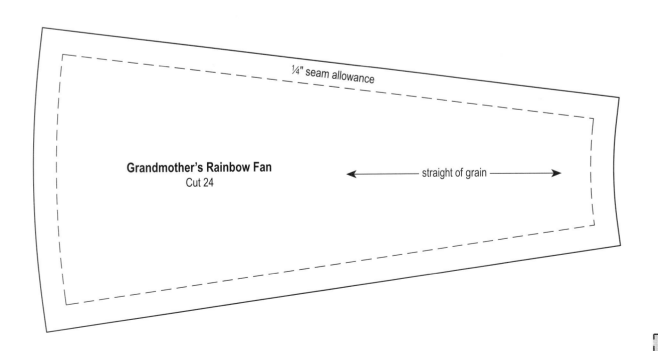

¼" seam allowance

Grandmother's Rainbow Fan
Cut 24

← straight of grain →

Hearts and Bow Ties

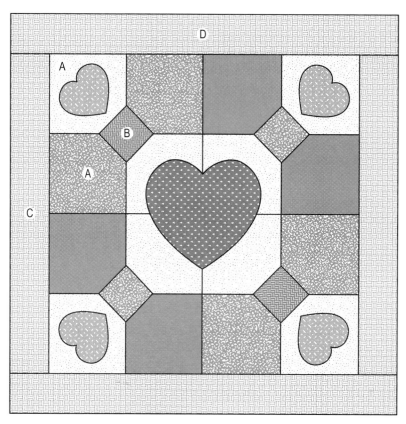

Quilt Size: 20" x 20" • Finished Block Size: 8" x 8"

Cream print   Light pink print   Floral print   Dark blue print

Medium pink print   Dark pink print   Light blue print

Materials (44"-wide fabric)

¼ yd. cream print
¼ yd. medium pink print
¼ yd. light pink print
⅛ yd. dark pink print
1 yd. floral print
⅛ yd. light blue print
Scrap of dark blue print
¾ yd. for backing
¼ yd. for binding
22" x 22" square of batting

Cutting

Use the heart templates on page 51.

From cream print, cut:
8 squares, each 4½" x 4½", for piece A

From medium pink print, cut:
4 squares, each 4½" x 4½", for piece A

From light pink print, cut:
4 squares, each 4½" x 4½", for piece A
2 squares, each 2½" x 2½", for piece B

From dark pink print, cut:
2 squares, each 2½" x 2½", for piece B

From floral print, cut:
2 strips, each 2½" x 16½", for piece C
2 strips, each 2½" x 20½", for piece D

From light blue print, cut:
4 small hearts, using the small heart
    template

From scrap of dark blue print, cut:
1 large heart, using the large heart template

From the backing fabric, cut:
1 square, 22" x 22"

Block Assembly

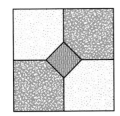

Bow Tie Block

1. Sew a cream print piece A square to a
   medium pink piece A square.

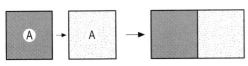

Make 4.

2. Sew 2 two-square units together to form
   a Four Patch.

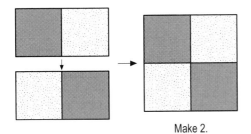

Make 2.

3. Referring to "Hand Appliqué," beginning on page 14, appliqué a light pink
   piece B square to the center of the block
   as shown.

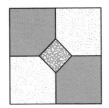

4. Follow steps 1–3 to make 2 more Bow
   Tie blocks, using light pink piece A
   squares and cream print piece A
   squares with dark pink piece B squares
   as shown.

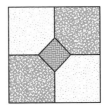

Make 2.

Quilt Top Assembly
1. Arrange the 4 Four Patch blocks as
   shown.

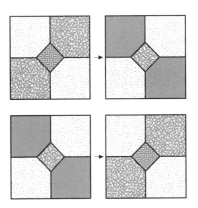

2. Sew the blocks together in pairs. Press the seam between one pair in one direction and the seam between the other pair in the opposite direction. Sew the pairs together. Press the seam to one side.

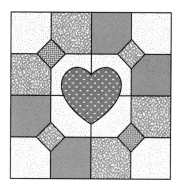

3. Following "Hand Appliqué," beginning on page 14, appliqué a large dark blue heart to the center of the blocks.

4. Appliqué a small light blue heart to each outer corner square.

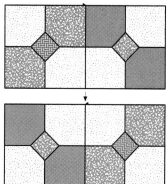

5. Sew a floral piece C strip to the sides of the quilt top. Press the seams toward the borders.

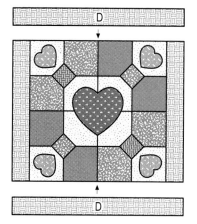

6. Sew a floral strip D to the top and bottom edges. Press the seams toward the borders.

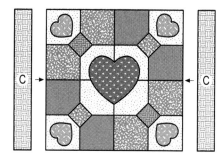

Finishing Touches

Refer to "Quilt Finishing Basics," beginning on page 15.

1. Layer the quilt top with batting and backing, and baste the layers together.
2. Quilt as shown in the diagram on page 51 or as desired.
3. Bind the edges.
4. Add a hanging sleeve.

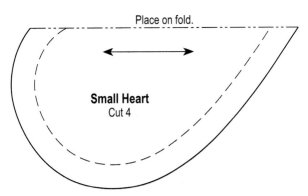

Place on fold.

Small Heart
Cut 4

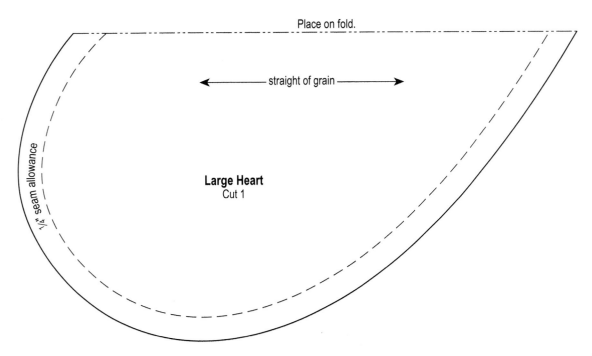

Place on fold.

straight of grain

Large Heart
Cut 1

¼" seam allowance

Leaves of the Season

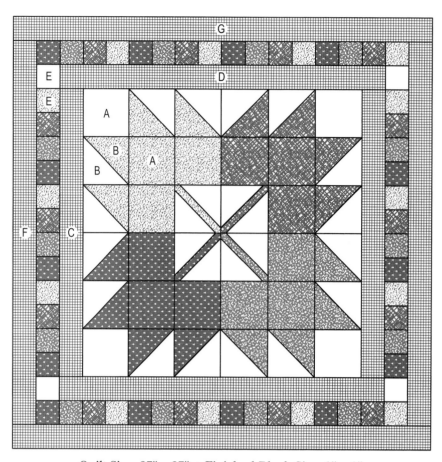

Quilt Size: 27" x 27" • Finished Block Size: 9" x 9"

Brown print   Gold print   Dark green print

Orange print   Cream print   Green check

Materials (44"-wide fabric)

¼ yd. brown print
¼ yd. orange print
1¼ yds. gold print for blocks and backing
¼ yd. cream print
¼ yd. dark green print
⅓ yd. green check for border
⅓ yd. for binding
29" x 29" square of batting

Cutting

From brown print, cut:

3 squares, each 3½" x 3½", for piece A
2 squares, each 3⅞" x 3⅞", cut once diagonally for 4 piece B
1 strip, 1½" x 4½", for stem
14 squares, each 2" x 2", for piece E

From orange print, cut:

3 squares, each 3½" x 3½", for piece A
2 squares, each 3⅞" x 3⅞", cut once diagonally for 4 piece B

1 strip, 1½" x 4½", for stem
14 squares, each 2" x 2", for piece E

From gold print, cut:
3 squares, each 3½" x 3½", for piece A
2 squares, each 3⅞" x 3⅞", cut once diagonally for 4 piece B
1 strip, 1½" x 4½", for stem
14 squares, each 2" x 2", for piece E

From cream print, cut:
8 squares, each 3½" x 3½", for piece A
8 squares, each 3⅞" x 3⅞", cut once diagonally for 4 piece B
4 squares, each 2" x 2", for piece E

From dark green print, cut:
3 squares, each 3½" x 3½", for piece A
2 squares, each 3⅞" x 3⅞", cut once diagonally for 4 piece B
1 strip, 1½" x 4½", for stem
14 squares, each 2" x 2", for piece E

From green checked fabric, cut:
2 strips, each 2" x 18½", for piece C
2 strips, each 2" x 21½", for piece D
2 strips, each 2" x 24½", for piece F
2 strips, each 2" x 27½", for piece G

From the gold print for backing, cut:
1 square, 29" x 29"

Block Assembly

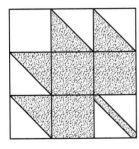

Leaf Block

1. Sew a gold piece B triangle to a cream piece B triangle along the diagonal edge to make half-square triangle units, being careful not to stretch the bias edges.

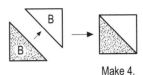

Make 4.

2. Fold the raw edges of the gold stem strip to meet at the center and baste along the folded edges.

3. With a pencil, draw a diagonal line on a cream piece A square. Center the stem along the line and pin or baste in place. Appliqué the stem to the cream square.

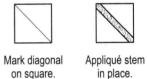

Mark diagonal on square.   Appliqué stem in place.

4. Arrange the stem square and the 4 gold-and-cream half-square triangle units with 3 gold piece A squares and 1 cream piece A square as shown.

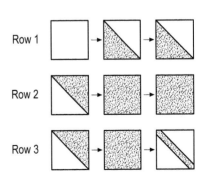

Row 1   Row 2   Row 3

5. Sew the squares together in rows. Press the seams of Rows 1 and 3 in one direction and the seams of Row 2 in the other direction.

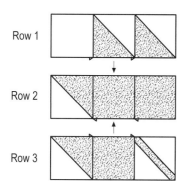

Row 1

Row 2

Row 3

6. Sew the rows together, taking care to match the seams.

7. Follow steps 1–6 to make 3 more blocks: 1 brown, 1 dark green, and 1 orange.

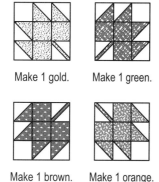

Make 1 gold.　Make 1 green.

Make 1 brown.　Make 1 orange.

Quilt Top Assembly

1. Referring to the quilt photo on page 30, arrange the Leaf blocks in pairs. Sew blocks together as shown. Press seams in opposite directions.

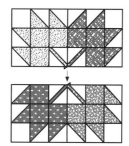

2. Sew the pairs of blocks together.

3. Sew a green checked piece C strip to each side of the patchwork. Press the seams toward the border.

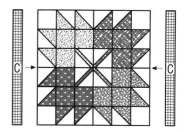

C → ← C

4. Sew a green checked piece D strip to the top and bottom of the patchwork. Press the seams toward the border.

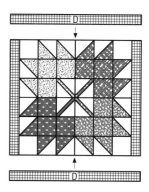

D

D

5. Arrange 14 piece E squares for each side border in the color sequence as shown. Arrange 16 pieces for the top and bottom borders. Sew the squares together to form the 4 pieced border strips.

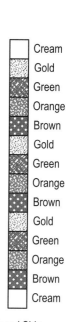

Cream
Gold
Green
Orange
Brown
Gold
Green
Orange
Brown
Gold
Green
Orange
Brown
Cream

Pieced Side
Borders
Make 2.

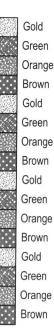

Gold
Green
Orange
Brown
Gold
Green
Orange
Brown
Gold
Green
Orange
Brown

Pieced Top and
Bottom Borders
Make 2.

6. Sew the pieced side border strips to the sides of the quilt. Press the seams toward the pieced border.

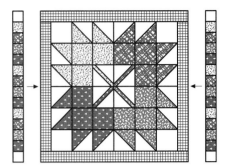

7. Sew the pieced top and bottom border strips to the top and bottom of the quilt. Press seams toward the inner border.

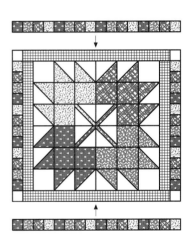

8. Add green checked piece F strips to the sides of the quilt top, then add piece G strips to the top and bottom. Press the seams toward the outer border.

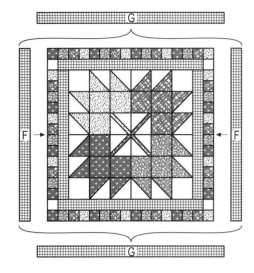

Finishing Touches

Refer to "Quilt Finishing Basics," beginning on page 15.

1. Layer the quilt top with batting and backing, and baste the layers together.
2. Quilt as shown in the diagram below or as desired.

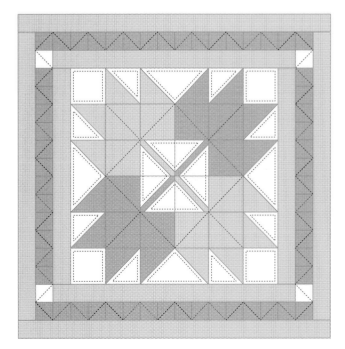

3. Bind the edges.
4. Add a hanging sleeve.

Londontown Roads

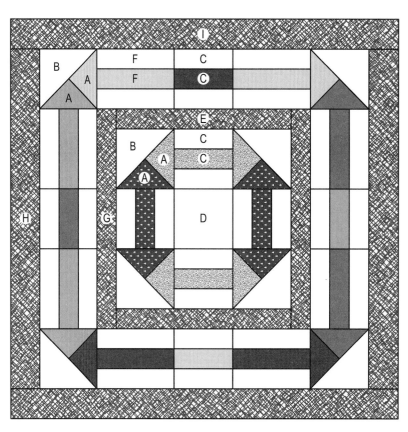

Quilt Size: 20" x 20" • Finished Block Size: 9" x 9"

Yellow print   Blue print #1   Pink solid   Yellow solid

Pink print   Blue print #2   Blue solid   Green solid

Materials (44"-wide fabric)

$1/3$ yd. yellow print
$1/8$ yd. pink print
$1/8$ yd. blue print #1
1 yd. blue print #2 for borders and backing
$1/8$ yd. pink solid
$1/8$ yd. blue solid
$1/8$ yd. yellow solid
$1/8$ yd. green solid
$1/4$ yd. for binding
22" x 22" square of batting

Cutting

From yellow print, cut:
4 squares, each $3^{7}/_{8}$" x $3^{7}/_{8}$", cut once diagonally for 8 piece B
1 square, $3^{1}/_{2}$" x $3^{1}/_{2}$", for piece D
16 rectangles, each $1^{1}/_{2}$" x $3^{1}/_{2}$", for piece C
16 rectangles, each $1^{1}/_{2}$" by $4^{1}/_{2}$", for piece F

From pink print, cut:
1 square, $4^{1}/_{4}$" x $4^{1}/_{4}$", cut twice diagonally for 4 piece A

2 rectangles, each 1½" x 3½", for piece C

From blue print #1, cut:
1 square, 4¼" x 4¼", cut twice diagonally for 4 piece A
2 rectangles, each 1½" x 3½", for piece C

From blue print #2, cut:
2 strips, each 1½" x 9½", for piece E
2 strips, each 1½" x 11½", for piece G
2 strips, each 2" x 17½", for piece H
2 strips, each 2" x 20½", for piece I
1 square, 22" x 22", for backing

From pink solid, cut:
1 square, 4¼" x 4¼", cut twice diagonally for 4 piece A
1 rectangle, 1½" x 3½", for piece C
2 rectangles, each 1½" x 4½", for piece F

From blue solid, cut:
1 square, 4¼" x 4¼", cut twice diagonally for 4 piece A
1 rectangle, 1½" x 3½", for piece C
2 rectangles, each 1½" x 4½", for piece F

From yellow solid, cut:
1 square, 4¼" x 4¼", cut twice diagonally for 4 piece A
1 rectangle, 1½" x 3½", for piece C
2 rectangles, each 1½" x 4½", for piece F

From green solid, cut:
1 square, 4¼" x 4¼", cut twice diagonally for 4 piece A
1 rectangle, 1½" x 3½", for piece C
2 rectangles, each 1½" x 4½", for piece F

Block Assembly

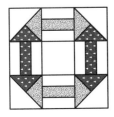

Londontown Roads Block

1. Sew a pink print piece A triangle to a blue print #1 piece A triangle as shown, being careful not to stretch the bias edges.

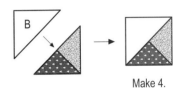

Make 4.

2. Sew a yellow print piece B triangle to the unit made in step 1.

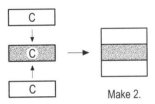

Make 4.

3. Sew a yellow print piece C rectangle to each side of a pink print piece C rectangle as shown.

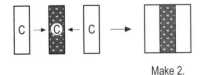

Make 2.

4. Sew a yellow print piece C rectangle to each side of a blue print #1 piece C rectangle as shown.

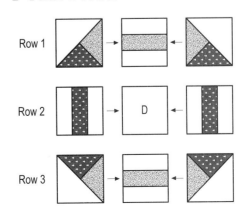

Make 2.

5. Arrange the pieced units made in steps 1–4 into 3 rows.

Row 1

Row 2

Row 3

6. Sew the units together into rows. Press the seams of Rows 1 and 3 in one direction and the seams of Row 2 in the opposite direction.

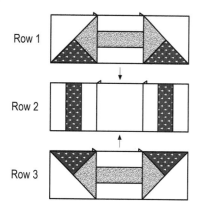

7. Sew the rows together, matching the seams between the units to complete the Londontown Roads block.

Quilt Top Assembly

1. Sew a blue print #2 piece E strip first to the top and bottom of the block, then a piece G to each side. Press the seams toward the border.

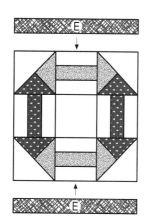

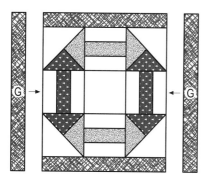

2. Sew together the piece A triangles to make 4 different corner units for the pieced border as shown.

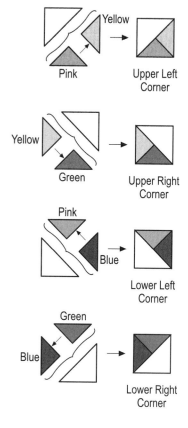

3. Using the yellow print piece F rectangles and the piece F rectangles cut from each solid color, make the following units.

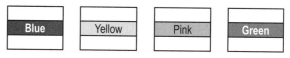

Make 2 with each solid color.

4. Using a yellow print piece C rectangle and the piece C rectangles cut from each solid color, make the following units.

Make 1 with each solid color.

5. Sew together the yellow and blue C and F units made in steps 3 and 4 as shown to make the top and bottom borders. Press the seams toward the ends of the border strips. Sew the border strips to the top and bottom of the quilt. Press the seams toward the outer border.

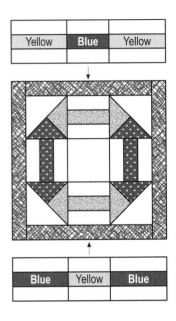

6. Using the pieced corner squares made in step 2, assemble the side border units as shown. Sew the units together. Press the seams toward the center of the strips.

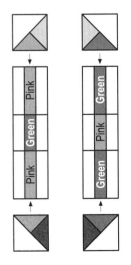

7. Sew the side border strips to the quilt top, matching the seams of the corner units and the top and bottom borders. Press seams toward the outer border.

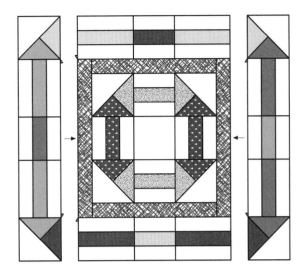

Finishing Touches

Refer to "Quilt Finishing Basics," beginning on page 15.

1. Layer the quilt top with batting and backing, and baste the layers together.
2. Quilt as shown in the diagram below or as desired.

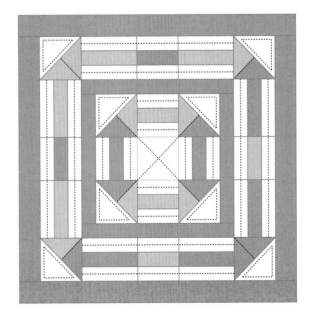

3. Bind the edges.
4. Add a hanging sleeve.

Needles and Spools

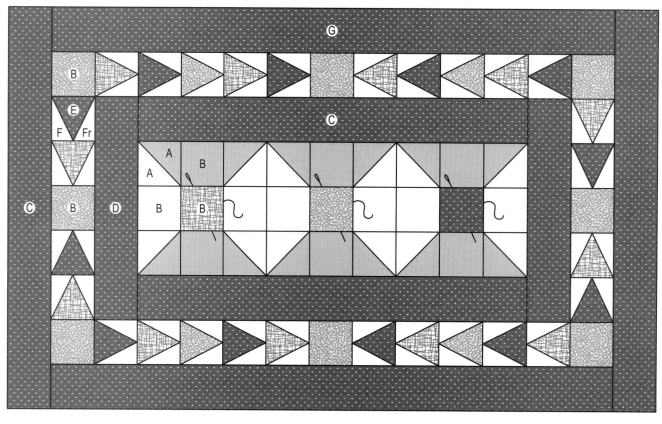

Quilt Size: 27" x 45" • Finished Block Sizes: Spool, 9" x 9" • Wild Goose Chase Unit, 3" x 3"

☐ Cream solid ▨ Red print ▨ Tan print

▨ Navy blue print ▨ Yellow print

Materials (44"-wide fabric)
$\frac{1}{2}$ yd. cream solid
1 yd. navy blue print
$\frac{1}{4}$ yd. red print
$\frac{1}{4}$ yd. yellow print
$\frac{1}{4}$ yd. tan print
$\frac{1}{2}$ yd. red print for binding
$1\frac{1}{2}$ yds. for backing
29" x 47" piece of batting
Embroidery thread: gray, red, yellow, blue

Cutting
Use Templates E and F on page 64.

From cream solid, cut:
6 squares, each $3\frac{7}{8}$" x $3\frac{7}{8}$", cut once diagonally for 12 piece A
6 squares, each $3\frac{1}{2}$" x $3\frac{1}{2}$", for piece B
56 triangles, using Template F for piece F

From navy blue print, cut:
1 square, $3\frac{1}{2}$" x $3\frac{1}{2}$", for piece B
4 strips, each $3\frac{1}{2}$" x $27\frac{1}{2}$", for piece C
2 strips, each $3\frac{1}{2}$" x $15\frac{1}{2}$", for piece D
12 triangles, using Template E for piece E
2 strips, each $3\frac{1}{2}$" x $39\frac{1}{2}$", for piece G

From red print, cut:
1 square, 3½" x 3½", for piece B
12 triangles, using Template E for piece E

From yellow print, cut:
9 squares, each 3½" x 3½", for piece B
4 triangles, using Template E for piece E

From tan print, cut:
6 squares, each 3⅞" x 3⅞", cut once diagonally for 12 piece A
6 squares, each 3½" x 3½", for piece B

From the backing fabric, cut:
1 rectangle, 29" x 47".

Spool Block Assembly

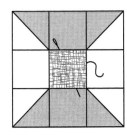

Spool Block

1. Sew a cream piece A triangle to a tan piece A triangle as shown to make half-square triangle units, being careful not to stretch the bias edges. Press the seam toward the tan triangle.

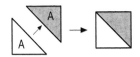

2. Arrange the half-square triangle units and piece B squares as shown in 3 rows of 3 pieces each.

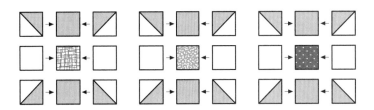

3. Sew the units together into rows. Press the seams of Rows 1 and 3 outward and the seams of Row 2 toward the center. Sew 3 rows together for each Spool block. Press the seams toward the bottom edges of the blocks.

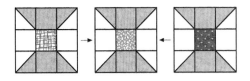

4. Sew the 3 Spool blocks together, matching the seams carefully and pressing the seams toward the ends of the row.

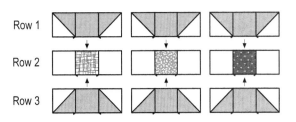

5. Sew a navy blue piece C strip to the top and bottom edges of the patchwork. Press the seams toward the border. Sew a navy blue piece D strip to the sides of the patchwork. Press the seams toward the border.

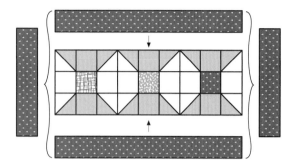

Wild Goose Chase Unit Assembly

1. Sew a cream piece F triangle to the 2 long sides of each print piece E triangle to make the Wild Goose Chase units.

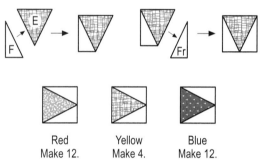

Red
Make 12.

Yellow
Make 4.

Blue
Make 12.

2. In this border design, the direction and color of the Wild Goose Chase units are important for achieving the look of the quilt. Arrange the units as shown. Sew them together to form the top and bottom pieced border strips.

3. Arrange the remaining Wild Goose Chase units and plain squares as shown. Sew them together to form the side pieced borders.

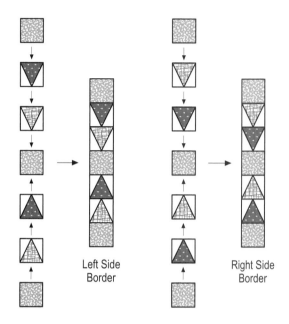

Left Side
Border

Right Side
Border

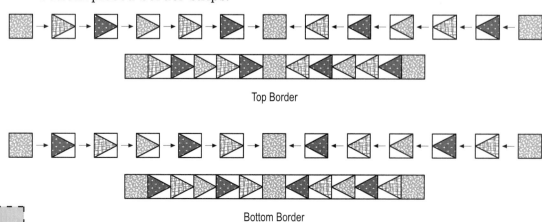

Top Border

Bottom Border

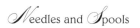
Quilt Top Assembly

1. Add top and bottom Wild Goose Chase border strips to the quilt top. Press the seams toward the pieced border.
2. Sew the side border strips to the sides of the quilt top, carefully matching the seams of the corner squares and the top and bottom borders. Press the seams toward the pieced border.

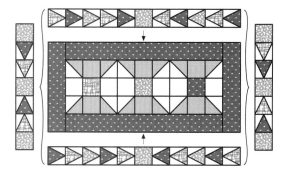

3. Sew a navy blue piece G strip to the top and bottom edges of the patchwork. Press seams toward the outer border.

4. Sew a navy blue piece C strip to each side of the patchwork. Press the seams toward the outer border.

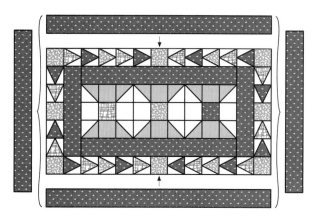

Finishing Touches

Refer to "Quilt Finishing Basics," beginning on page 15.

1. Mark a scalloped quilting design on the C, D, G, and H strips as shown in the diagram on page 64. Trace the needle and thread motif from page 64 onto the Spool blocks and embroider with the appropriate color thread, using a backstitch.
2. Layer the quilt top with the batting and backing, and baste the layers together.
3. Quilt as shown in the diagram on page 64 or as desired.
4. Bind the edges.
5. Add a hanging sleeve.

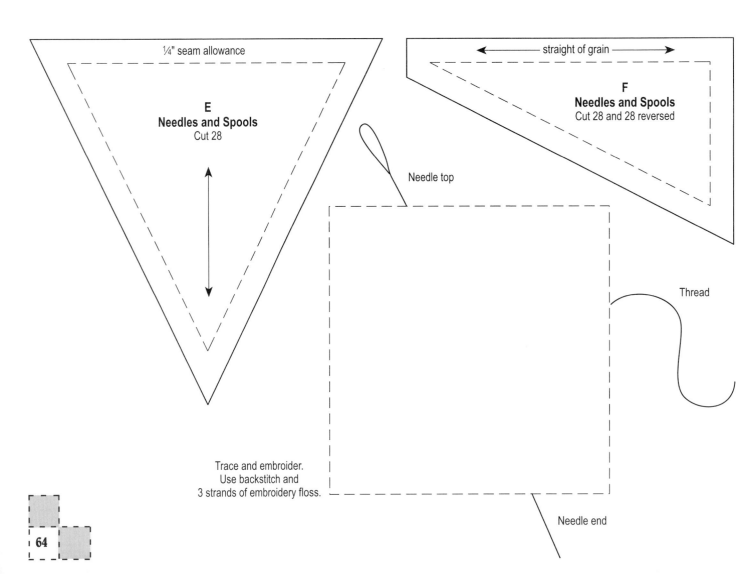

¼" seam allowance

E
Needles and Spools
Cut 28

straight of grain

F
Needles and Spools
Cut 28 and 28 reversed

Needle top

Thread

Trace and embroider.
Use backstitch and
3 strands of embroidery floss.

Needle end

Ninepatch Sampler

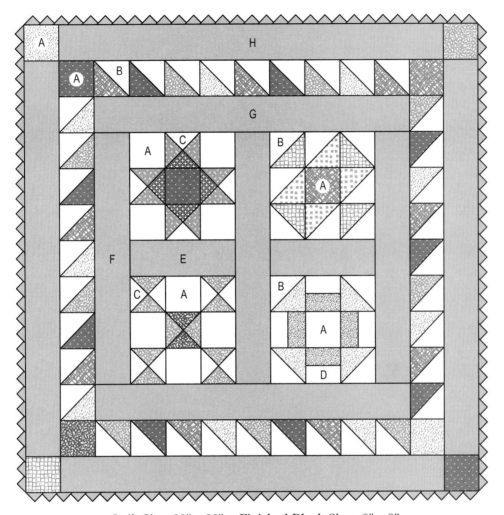

Quilt Size: 39" x 39" • Finished Block Size: 9" x 9"

☐ White solid	▨ Dark peach print	▨ Dark pink print	▨ Light purple print
▨ Medium peach print	▨ Medium yellow print	▨ Medium pink print	▨ Dark purple print
▨ Light peach print	▨ Dark yellow print	▨ Medium purple print	▨ Aqua print

Materials (44"-wide fabric)

1 yd. white solid
¼ yd. medium peach print
⅛ yd. light peach print
⅛ yd. dark peach print
⅛ yd. medium yellow print
⅛ yd. dark yellow print
⅛ yd. medium pink print

⅛ yd. dark pink print
⅛ yd. medium purple print
⅛ yd. light purple print
⅛ yd. dark purple print
1¼ yds. aqua print for borders and prairie
   points
1¼ yds. for backing
41" x 41" square of batting

Cutting

From white fabric, cut:

9 squares, each 3½" x 3½", for piece A

20 squares, each 3⅞" x 3⅞", cut once diagonally for 40 piece B

4 rectangles, each 2" x 3½", for piece D

3 squares, each 4¼" x 4¼", cut twice diagonally for 12 piece C

From medium peach print, cut:

1 square, 3½" x 3½", for piece A

7 squares, 3⅞" x 3⅞", cut once diagonally for 14 piece B

From light peach print, cut:

2 squares, each 3⅞" x 3⅞", cut once diagonally for 4 piece B

From dark peach print, cut:

2 squares, 3½" x 3½", for piece A

From medium yellow print, cut:

7 squares, each 3⅞" x 3⅞", cut once diagonally for 14 piece B

2 squares, each 3½" x 3½", for piece A

From dark yellow print, cut:

4 rectangles, each 2" x 3½", for piece D

From medium pink print, cut:

6 squares, each 3⅞" x 3⅞", cut once diagonally for 12 piece B

3 squares, each 4¼" x 4¼", cut twice diagonally for 12 piece C

From dark pink print, cut:

1 square, 3½" x 3½", for piece A

1 square, 4¼" x 4¼", cut twice diagonally for 4 piece C

From medium purple print, cut:

2 squares, each 3½" x 3½", for piece A

5 squares, each 3⅞" x 3⅞", cut once diagonally for 10 piece B

From light purple print, cut:

2 squares, each 4¼" x 4¼", cut twice diagonally for 8 piece C

From dark purple print, cut:

1 square, 4¼" x 4¼", cut twice diagonally for 4 piece C

From aqua print, cut:

2 strips, each 3½" x 9½", for piece E

3 strips, each 3½" x 21½", for piece F

2 strips, each 3½" x 27½", for piece G

4 strips, each 3½" x 33½", for piece H

75 squares, each 3½" x 3½", for prairie points

From the backing fabric, cut:

1 square, 41" x 41".

Box Kite Block Assembly

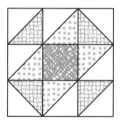

Box Kite Block

1. Sew a medium peach piece B triangle to a white piece B triangle, and a light peach piece B triangle to a white piece B triangle along the long sides, being careful not to stretch the bias edges. Press the seams toward the peach triangles.

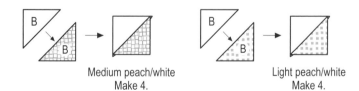

Medium peach/white
Make 4.

Light peach/white
Make 4.

2. Arrange the half-square triangle units together with a dark peach piece A square into 3 rows of 3.

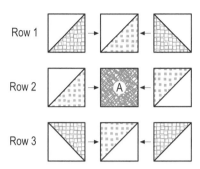

3. Sew the units together into rows. Press the seams of Rows 1 and 3 in one direction and the seams of Row 2 in the opposite direction.

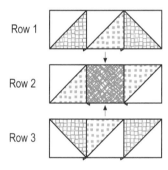

4. Sew the rows together to form the Box Kite block.

Churn Dash Block Assembly

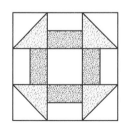

Churn Dash Block

1. Sew a medium yellow piece B triangle to a white piece B triangle along the

diagonal edge. Press the seam toward the yellow triangle.

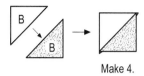

Make 4.

2. Sew a dark yellow piece D rectangle to a white piece D rectangle. Press the seam toward the yellow rectangle.

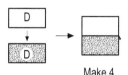

Make 4.

3. Arrange the half-square triangle units and the strip units as shown. Sew them together into rows. Press the seams of Rows 1 and 3 inward and the seams of Row 2 outward.

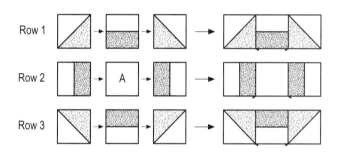

4. Sew the rows together to form the Churn Dash block.

Clown's Choice Block Assembly

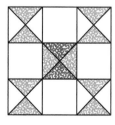

Clown's Choice Block

1. Sew a medium pink piece C triangle to a white piece C triangle along the short

sides, being careful not to stretch the bias edges. Press seams toward the pink triangle.

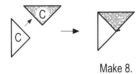

Make 8.

2. Sew pairs of triangle units together to form the Hourglass unit as shown.

Make 4.

3. Sew a dark pink piece C triangle to a medium pink piece C triangle along the short sides, being careful not to stretch the bias edges. Press the seam toward the dark pink triangle.

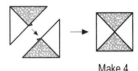

Make 2.

4. Sew the triangle units together to make an Hourglass unit.

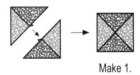

Make 1.

5. Arrange the Hourglass units and white piece A squares together into rows as shown.

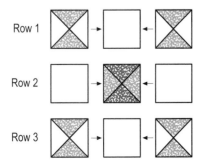

6. Sew the units together into rows. Press the seams of Rows 1 and 3 outward and the seams of Row 2 inward.

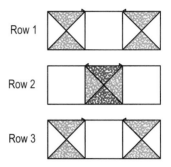

7. Sew the rows together to form the Clown's Choice block.

Ohio Star Block Assembly

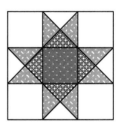

Ohio Star Block

1. Sew a light purple piece C triangle to a white piece C triangle, and a dark purple piece C triangle to a light purple piece C triangle. Press seams toward the light purple triangles.

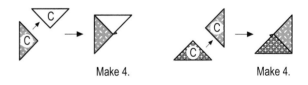

Make 4.   Make 4.

2. Sew the triangle units together as shown to make an Hourglass unit.

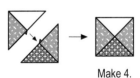

Make 4.

3. Arrange the Hourglass units together with a medium purple piece A square and 3 white piece A squares in rows as shown.

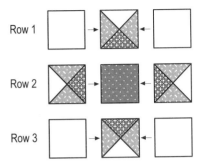

4. Sew the units together into rows. Press the seams of Rows 1 and 3 in toward the center and the seams of Row 2 in the opposite direction.

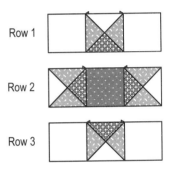

5. Sew the rows together to form the Ohio Star block.

Quilt Top Assembly

1. Arrange the 4 blocks as shown and sew aqua piece E strips between the 2 blocks on the right and between the 2 blocks on the left. Press the seams toward the aqua strips.

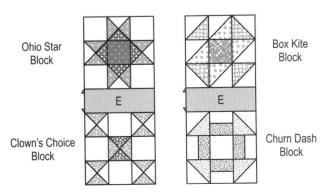

2. Add an aqua piece F strip between the sets of blocks and one on each side of the blocks, then add piece G strips to the top and bottom edges as shown.

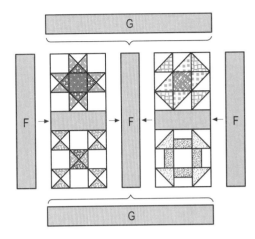

3. Sew together white piece B triangles with colored piece B triangles to form the following half-square triangles.

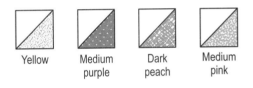

4. Sew the units together with piece A squares to form sawtooth pieced border strips.

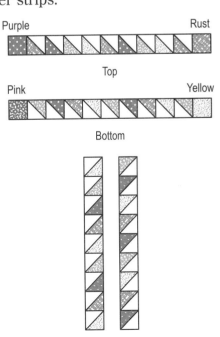

5. Add the pieced border strips to the sides of the quilt top, then to the top and bottom. Press the seams toward the pieced border.

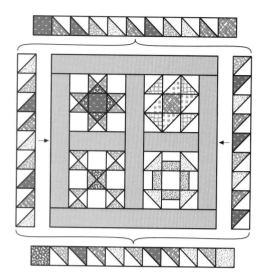

6. Sew an aqua piece H strip to each side of the patchwork.

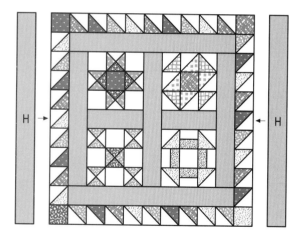

7. Sew piece A squares to the ends of the aqua top and bottom outer border strips (H) as shown. Press the seams toward the border strips. Sew the border strips to the quilt top, matching the corner-square seams with the side border seams. Press the seams toward the outer border.

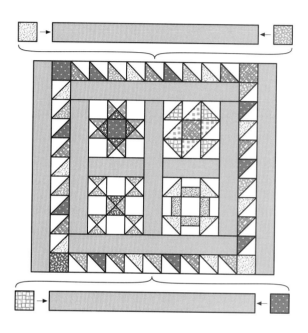

Finishing Touches

Refer to "Quilt Finishing Basics," beginning on page 15.

1. From the 3½" aqua squares, make a prairie-point edging and sew the points to the edges of the quilt top. (See instructions on page 15.)

2. Layer the quilt top with batting and backing and baste the layers together.

3. Mark the patchwork quilt top with heart motifs as shown in the quilt plan.

4. Quilt as shown in the diagram below or as desired.

5. Carefully trim the edges of the batting and backing to ¼" from the quilt-top edge. Turn the edges of the backing under and stitch the backing to the base of the prairie points.

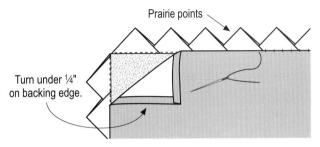

Hand stitch backing to base of prairie points.

6. Add a hanging sleeve.

Pinwheels and Posies

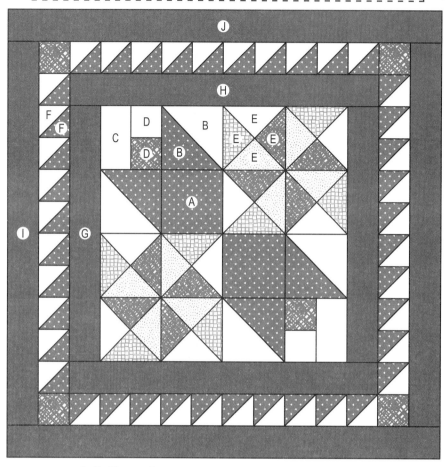

Quilt Size: 28" x 28" • Finished Block Sizes: 8" x 8"

White solid

Dark purple print #1

Medium purple print

Light purple print

Dark turquoise print

Cream print

Materials (44"-wide fabric)
1/3 yd. white solid

1 yd. dark purple print #1 for borders and backing

1/3 yd. medium purple print

1/8 yd. light purple print

1/4 yd. dark turquoise print

1/8 yd. cream print

1/3 yd. dark purple print #2 for binding

30" x 30" square of batting

Cutting
From white solid, cut:

2 squares, each 4⁷/₈" x 4⁷/₈", cut once diagonally for 4 piece B

2 rectangles, each 2¹/₂" x 4¹/₂", for piece C

2 squares, each 2¹/₂" x 2¹/₂", for piece D

2 squares, each 5¹/₄" x 5¹/₄", cut twice diagonally for 8 piece E

20 squares, each 2⁷/₈" x 2⁷/₈", cut once diagonally for 40 piece F

From dark purple print #1, cut:

2 strips, each 2¹/₂" x 16¹/₂", for piece G

2 strips, each 2¹/₂" x 20¹/₂", for piece H

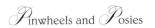
2 strips, each 2½" x 24½", for piece I
2 strips, each 2½" x 28½", for piece J
1 square, 30" x 30", for backing

From medium purple print, cut:
2 squares, each 4½" x 4½", for piece A
2 squares, each 4⅞" x 4⅞", cut once diagonally for 4 piece B
20 squares, each 2⅞" x 2⅞", cut once diagonally for 40 piece F

From light purple print, cut:
2 squares, each 5¼" x 5¼", cut twice diagonally for 8 piece E

From dark turquoise print, cut:
6 squares, each 2½" x 2½", for piece D
2 squares, each 5¼" x 5¼", cut twice diagonally for 8 piece E

From cream print, cut:
2 squares, each 5¼" x 5¼", cut twice diagonally for 8 piece E

Pinwheel Block Assembly

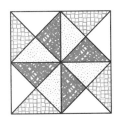

Pinwheel Block

1. Sew a light purple piece E triangle to a white piece E triangle, and a turquoise piece E triangle to a cream piece E triangle, along the short sides, being careful not to stretch the bias edges. Press the seams toward the darker fabric.

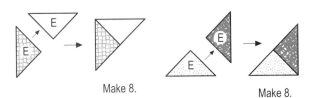

Make 8.   Make 8.

2. Sew the triangle pairs together as shown to form pieced squares.

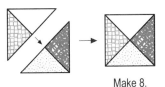

Make 8.

3. Arrange the pieced squares in 2 rows of 2. Then sew the rows together. Press the seams of one pair in one direction and the seams of the other pair in the opposite direction.

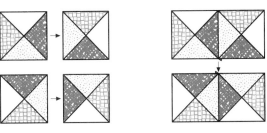

Make 2.

Posy Block Assembly

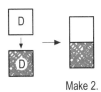

Posy Block

1. Sew a white piece D square to a dark turquoise piece D square.

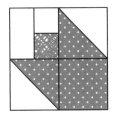

Make 2.

2. Sew a white piece C rectangle to the left side of the D unit.

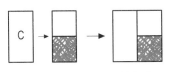

Make 2.

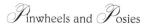
3. Sew a white piece B triangle to a medium purple piece B triangle along the long sides, taking care not to stretch the bias edges.

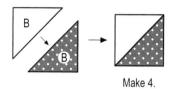

Make 4.

4. Arrange the units as shown below and sew them together. Press the seam of one pair in one direction and the seam of the other pair in the opposite direction.

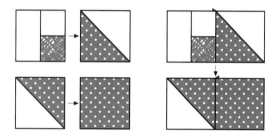

Quilt Top Assembly

1. Sew the 2 Posy blocks and the 2 Pinwheel blocks together as shown. Press the seams between the pairs in opposing directions.

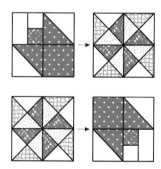

2. Add dark purple #1 piece G strips to the sides of the quilt, then add dark purple #1 piece H strips to the top and bottom. Press the seams toward the borders.

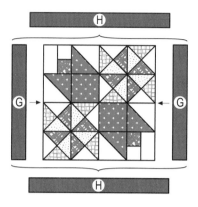

3. Sew a medium purple piece F triangle to a white piece F triangle along the long sides to make a sawtooth unit. Press the seam toward the purple triangle.

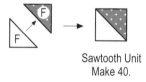

Sawtooth Unit
Make 40.

4. Sew together sawtooth units to make border strips as shown. Add a dark turquoise piece D square to each end of the side borders. Press the seams toward the ends of the border strips.

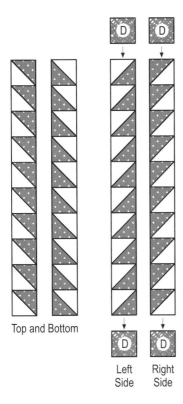

Top and Bottom

Left Side   Right Side

5. Sew sawtooth border strips to the top and bottom of the quilt top. Then, sew sawtooth borders to the sides of the quilt top, matching the corner-square seams with the top and bottom border seams. Press the seams toward the inner border.

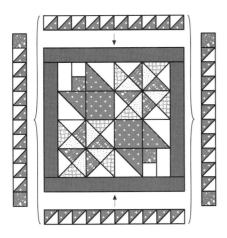

6. Sew piece I strips to the sides of the quilt top, then sew piece J strips to the top and bottom. Press the seams toward the outer border.

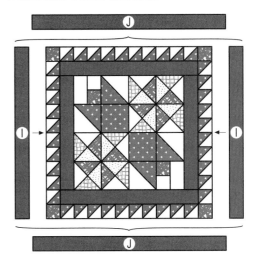

Finishing Touches

Refer to "Quilt Finishing Basics," beginning on page 15.

1. Layer the quilt top with the batting and backing, and baste the layers together.
2. Quilt as shown in the diagram below or as desired.

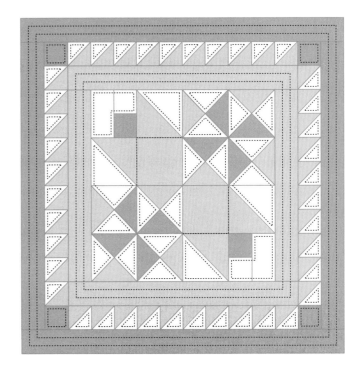

3. Bind the edges.
4. Add a hanging sleeve.

Sailboat and Fish

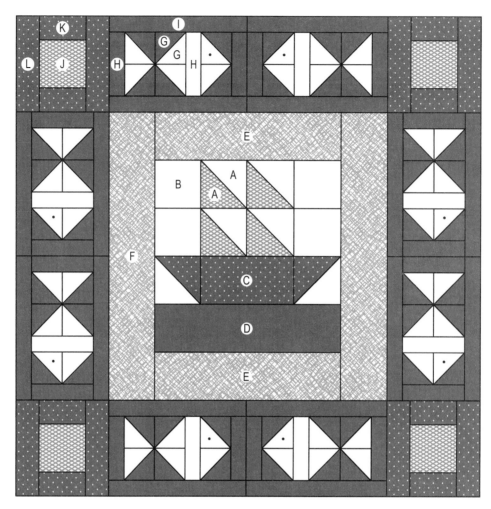

Quilt Size: 30" x 30" • Finished Block Sizes: Sailboat, 12" x 12" • Fish, 6" x 9"

■ Navy blue print   ▨ Medium green check   ▨ Light green print

▨ Dark green print   □ White/blue pindot

Materials (44"-wide fabric)
⅝ yd. navy blue print
¼ yd. dark green print
¼ yd. medium green check
¼ yd. white/blue pindot
⅛ yd. light green print
1 yd. for backing
⅓ yd. for binding
Dark green embroidery thread
32" x 32" square of batting

Cutting
From navy blue print, cut:
1 rectangle, 3½" x 12½", for
  piece D
24 squares, each 2⅞" x 2⅞", for
  piece G*
16 rectangles, each 1½" x 4½", for
  piece H
16 rectangles, each 1½" x 9½", for
  piece I

From dark green print, cut:
1 square, 3⅞" x 3⅞", cut once diagonally
  for 2 piece A
1 rectangle, 3½" x 12½", for piece C
8 rectangles, each 2" x 3½", for piece K
8 rectangles, each 2" x 6½", for piece L

From medium green checked fabric, cut:
2 squares, each 3⅞" x 3⅞", cut once diagonally for 4 piece A
4 squares, each 3½" x 3½", for piece J

From white/blue pindot, cut:
3 squares, each 3⅞" x 3⅞", cut once diagonally for 6 piece A
4 squares, each 3½" x 3½", for piece B
24 squares, each 2⅞" by 2⅞", cut once diagonally for 48 piece G
8 rectangles, each 1½" x 4½", for piece H

From light green print, cut:
2 rectangles, each 3½" x 12½", for piece E
2 rectangles, each 3½" x 18½", for piece F

From the backing fabric, cut:
1 square, 32" x 32".

Sailboat Block Assembly

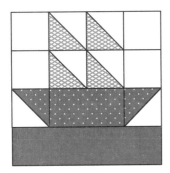

Sailboat Block

1. Sew a white/blue pindot piece A to a
   medium green piece A triangle along
   the long sides, being careful not to
   stretch the bias edges. Sew a white/
   blue pindot piece A triangle to a dark
   green piece A triangle along the long

sides. Press the seams toward the
darker triangle.

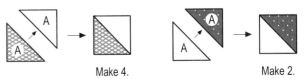

Make 4.   Make 2.

2. Arrange the half-square triangle units
   made in step 1 with 4 white/blue pindot
   piece B squares and the dark green
   piece C rectangle as shown.

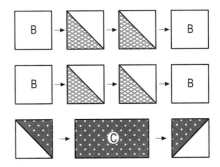

3. Sew the units together into rows. Press
   the seams of Rows 1 and 3 in one direction and the seams of Row 2 in the opposite direction.

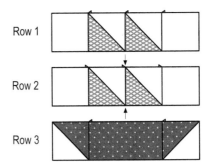

4. Sew a navy blue piece D rectangle to
   the bottom edge of the block. Press the
   seam toward the edge of the block.

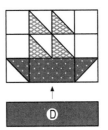

5. Sew a light green piece E rectangle to the top and bottom edges of the patchwork block. Press toward the edge of the block. Sew a medium green piece F rectangle to the sides of the patchwork. Press toward the edge of the block.

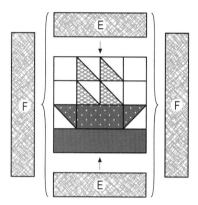

Fish Block Border Assembly

1. Sew a white/blue pindot piece G triangle to a navy blue piece G triangle along the long edge to make half-square triangle units. Press the seam toward the darker triangle.

Make 48.

2. Sew pairs of half-square triangle units together and add navy blue and white piece H rectangles as shown.

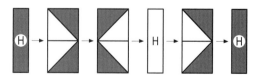

3. Sew navy blue piece I rectangles to the top and bottom edges of the block. Add a French knot for the fish's eye.

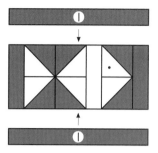

4. To make the corner blocks, sew dark green piece K rectangles to the top and bottom edges of the medium green piece J squares. Then sew dark green piece L rectangles to the sides.

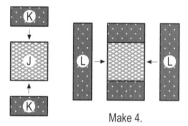

Make 4.

5. Arrange the Fish and corner blocks into 4 border strips as shown: 2 with fish facing each other and 2 with fish facing one direction (or arrange as desired). Sew the blocks together. Press the seams toward the Fish blocks.

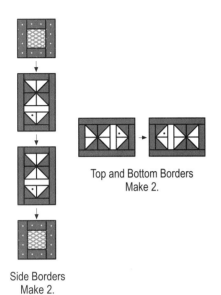

Top and Bottom Borders
Make 2.

Side Borders
Make 2.

6. Sew pieced border strips to the top and bottom, then to the sides of the quilt top, matching the seams of the corner blocks to the top and bottom border seams. Press the seams toward the pieced borders.

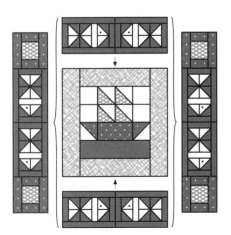

Finishing Touches

Refer to "Quilt Finishing Basics," beginning on page 15.

1. Layer the quilt top with batting and backing, and baste the layers together.
2. Quilt as shown in the diagram below or as desired.

3. Bind the edges.
4. Add a hanging sleeve or hanging rings.

Stars and Stripes

Quilt Size: 24" x 24" • Finished Block Size: 8" x 8"

■ Dark red print	▨ Dark navy blue print #2	░ Light navy blue print
▦ Dark navy blue print #1	□ White solid	▥ Red-and-white stripe

Materials (44"-wide fabric)
1½ yds. dark red print for blocks, borders, backing, and binding
¼ yd. dark navy blue print #1
¼ yd. dark navy blue print #2
¼ yd. white solid
⅛ yd. light navy blue print
⅛ yd. red-and-white stripe
26" x 26" square of batting

Cutting
From the dark red print, cut:
12 squares, each 2⅞" x 2⅞", cut once diagonally for 24 piece A
4 squares, each 2½" x 2½", for piece B
2 squares, each 4½" x 4½", for piece C
1 square, 26" x 26", for backing

From dark navy blue print #1, cut:
4 squares, each 2⅞" x 2⅞", cut once diagonally for 8 piece A

4 rectangles, each 2½" x 8½", for
   piece D

From dark navy blue print #2, cut:
2 strips, each 2½" x 20½", for piece F
2 strips, each 2½" x 24½", for piece G

From white solid, cut:
8 squares, each 2⅞" x 2⅞", cut once diagonally for 16 piece A
8 squares, each 2½" x 2½", for piece B

From light navy blue print, cut:
4 rectangles, each 2½" x 8½", for
   piece D

From red/white striped fabric, cut:
4 rectangles, each 2½" x 12½", for
   piece E

Star Block Assembly

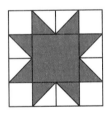

Star Block

1. Sew a dark red piece A triangle to a
   white piece A triangle along the long
   sides, being careful not to stretch the
   bias edges. Press toward the dark red
   triangle. Sew 2 of these units together,
   carefully noting color placement as
   shown. Press to one side.

Make 16.   Make 8.

2. Sew half-square triangle units
   to the top and bottom edges
   of a dark red piece C center
   square. Press the seams toward the square.

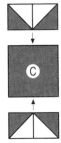

3. Make side units by adding a
   white piece B square to each end
   of a double half-square triangle
   unit. Press the seams toward the
   center of the strip.

Make 4.

4. Sew a side unit to each side of a center-
   square unit as shown. Press seams toward the center.

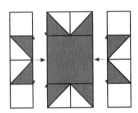

Stripe Block Assembly

Sew dark navy blue #1 and light navy blue
piece D rectangles together as shown.

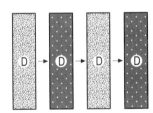

Quilt Top Assembly

1. Sew Star blocks to Striped blocks in
   pairs as shown. Press the seam of one
   pair in one direction and the seam of
   the other pair in the opposite direction.
   Sew pairs together, matching seams.

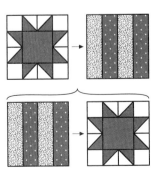

2. Sew a dark navy blue #1 piece A triangle to a dark red piece A triangle along the long sides as shown, being careful not to stretch the bias edges.

Make 8.

3. Assemble borders as shown and sew the units together. Press the seams toward the centers of the strips.

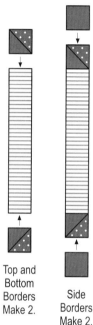

Top and Bottom Borders Make 2.

Side Borders Make 2.

4. Sew the top and bottom borders to the quilt. Press seams toward the borders. Sew side borders to the quilt, matching the seams of the corner squares to the top and bottom border seams. Press seams toward the borders.

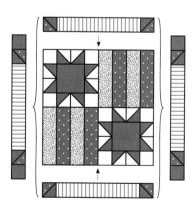

5. Sew a dark navy blue #2 piece F strip to the top and bottom of the quilt top. Press the seams toward the outer borders. Sew a dark navy blue #2 piece G strip to either side of the quilt top. Press seams toward the outer border.

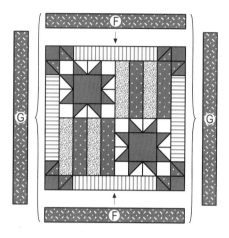

Finishing Touches

Refer to "Quilt Finishing Basics," beginning on page 15.

1. Layer the quilt top with batting and backing, and baste the layers together.
2. Quilt as shown in the diagram below or as desired.

3. Bind the edges.
4. Add a hanging sleeve.

Tumbling Baskets

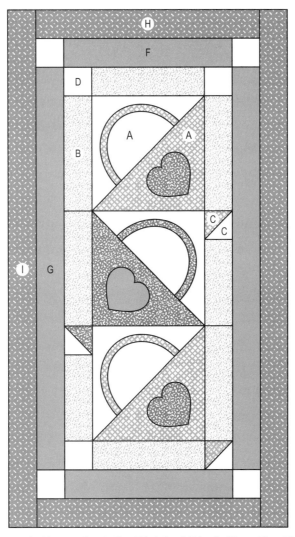

Quilt Size: 20" x 36" • Finished Block Size: 8" x 8"

- ☐ White solid
- ▨ Medium pink print
- ▨ Dark pink print
- ▨ Light green print
- ▨ Medium green print
- ▨ Dark green print

Materials (44"-wide fabric)
$\frac{1}{2}$ yd. white solid
$\frac{7}{8}$ yd. medium pink print for blocks and
    binding
$\frac{1}{3}$ yd. dark pink print
$\frac{1}{4}$ yd. light green print
$\frac{1}{4}$ yd. medium green print
$\frac{1}{3}$ yd. dark green print
$1\frac{1}{4}$ yds. for backing
22" x 38" piece of batting

Cutting
From white solid, cut:
2 squares, each $8\frac{7}{8}$" x $8\frac{7}{8}$", cut once diagonally for 4 piece A
2 squares, each $2\frac{7}{8}$" x $2\frac{7}{8}$", cut once diagonally for 4 piece C
7 squares, each $2\frac{1}{2}$" x $2\frac{1}{2}$", for piece D

From medium pink print, cut:
1 square, $8\frac{7}{8}$" x $8\frac{7}{8}$", cut once diagonally for 2 piece A

1 square, 2⅞" x 2⅞", cut once diagonally
for 2 piece C

From dark pink print, cut:
2 strips, each 2½" x 12½", for piece F
2 strips, each 2½" x 28½", for piece G
1 heart, using the appliqué template on
page 86

From light green print, cut:
6 strips, each 2½" x 8½", for piece B
2 strips, each 2½" x 6½", for piece E

From medium green print, cut:
2 strips, each 2½" x 16½", for piece H
2 strips, each 2½" x 36½", for piece I

From dark green print, cut:
1 square, 8⅞" x 8⅞", cut once diagonally
for 2 piece A
1 square, 2⅞" x 2⅞", cut once diagonally
for 2 piece C
2 hearts, using the appliqué template on
page 86

From the backing fabric, cut:
1 rectangle, 22" x 38".

Block Assembly

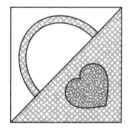

1. Cut 1 dark green and 2 medium pink
   bias strips, each 1½" x 11½", for the
   handles.

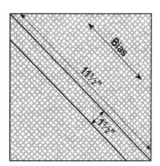

2. Fold the handle strips in half lengthwise with wrong sides together and
   stitch ¼" from the edge. Press the ¼"-
   wide seam allowance under, creating
   ¾"-wide strips.

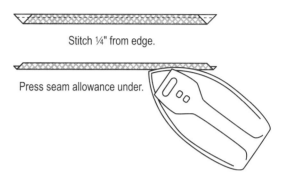

Stitch ¼" from edge.

Press seam allowance under.

3. Appliqué a handle to a white piece A
   triangle. Be sure each handle end is
   2½" from the side triangle corner and
   that the center arch is 2" from the top
   corner.

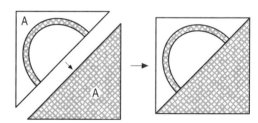

4. Sew a white piece A triangle with a
   handle to the colored piece A triangle
   that matches the handle. Make 3 Basket blocks: 2 medium pink and 1 dark
   green.

5. Appliqué a heart to each basket: dark
   green on the medium pink baskets and
   dark pink on the dark green basket.

Quilt Top Assembly

1. Sew together the 3 Basket blocks. Press the seams toward the darker fabric.

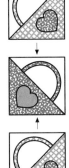

2. Sew a white piece C triangle to each of the 2 medium pink piece C triangles and to the 1 dark green piece C triangle, to make half-square triangle units as shown.

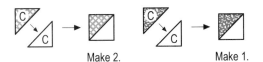

Make 2.   Make 1.

3. Arrange the half-square triangle units with the light green piece B and piece E strips and the white piece D squares to form the side inner border strips.

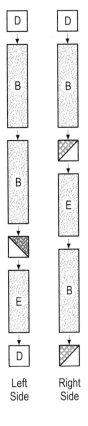

Left Side   Right Side

4. Sew a light green piece B strip to the top and bottom of the quilt. Press the seams toward the borders. Sew the side inner border strips made in step 3 to the side edges of the blocks. Press the seams toward the border.

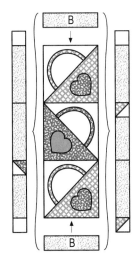

5. Sew dark pink piece F strips to the top and bottom of the quilt top. Press the seams toward the middle border.

6. Sew white piece D squares to the ends of the 2 dark pink piece G strips. Sew the strips to the sides of the quilt top, matching the corner-square seams with the top and bottom border seams. Press seams toward the middle border.

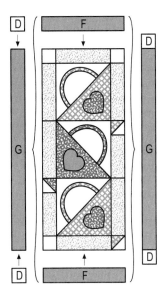

7. Sew medium green piece H strips to the top and bottom edges of the quilt top. Then, add the medium green piece I strips to the sides of the quilt top. Press seams toward the outer border.

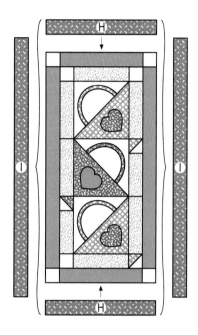

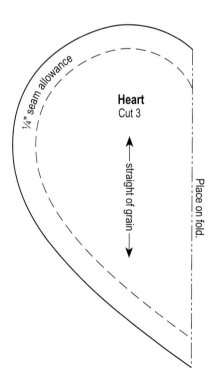

Heart
Cut 3

¼" seam allowance

straight of grain

Place on fold.

Finishing Touches

Refer to "Quilt Finishing Basics," beginning on page 15.

1. Layer the quilt top with batting and backing, and baste the layers together.
2. Quilt as shown in the diagram below or as desired.

3. Bind the edges.
4. Add a hanging sleeve.

About the Author

A lover of quilts since she was a child and a designer for over twenty years, Eileen Westfall is the author of numerous magazine articles and seven books on quilting. She currently lives with her husband, John, son Damian, and their cocker spaniel, Josey, in an old Cape Cod–style house filled with quilts in Walnut Creek, California. She teaches quilting at Thimble Creek Quilt Shop and is a member of Diablo Valley Quilters.

That Patchwork Place Publications and Products

4", 6", 8", & metric Bias Square® • BiRangle™ • Ruby Beholder™ • Pineapple Rule • ScrapMaster • Rotary Rule™ • Rotary Mate™
Shortcuts to America's Best-Loved Quilts (video)

Many titles are available at your local quilt shop. For more information, send $2 for a color catalog to
That Patchwork Place, Inc., PO Box 118, Bothell WA 98041-0118 USA.

☎ Call 1-800-426-3126 for the name and location of the quilt shop nearest you.